VEILED THREAT

WILLEM KOOMAN

authorHOUSE®

AuthorHouse™
1663 Liberty Drive
Bloomington, IN 47403
www.authorhouse.com
Phone: 1-800-839-8640

First published by AuthorHouse 4/26/2011

ISBN: 978-1-4567-6090-8 (e)
ISBN: 978-1-4567-6092-2 (dj)
ISBN: 978-1-4567-6091-5 (sc)

Library of Congress Control Number: 2011906509

Printed in the United States of America

Unless otherwise indicated, Bible quotations are taken from The Life Application Study Bible, New International Version of the Bible, ©1991 *by Zondervan*

Unless otherwise indicated, quotations from the Quran are taken from Muhammad Zafrulla Khan's translation, ©1997 by Olive Branch Press

to those who dare to question and seek the truth
and speak it boldly without fear

TABLE OF CONTENTS

* Chapter Twelve and Chapter Thirteen, new chapters, for the Second Edition

FOREWORD

INTRO:

When I first sat down to learn more about Islam, as I outlined in the first edition of *Veiled Threat*, I did so simply out of interest, as an attempt to better understand the worldwide religion. Little did I know that I would discover a religion whose roots sprung from a seedbed very different than the Judeo-Christian bedrock. Instead I became convinced this global faith is founded by Satanic evil that has enslaved one third of the world's population and seeks to control the remaining masses under its powerful and never-ending agenda of pernicious hatred and depravity.

When I started writing I never expected to use such strong and clear language to describe a religion many often announce, from pulpits and platforms, houses of government and houses of prayer, as a "religion of peace." It was only when I attended a recent conference in Ontario, Canada, when I heard the sort of strong language I now use spoken by a man with an inside look at the religion itself.

Sam Solomon confirmed what I discovered through the oftentimes gruelling and lonely hours of research I spent to explore the reality of Islam. The horrific footage I had seen of beheadings and atrocities captured on film by Muslims with loud shouts of Allah Akbar, along with the written accounts of Islamic leaders and teachers, and the spellbinding stories of Muslims who escaped or left Islam, became a breathing reality in the person of Sam Solomon.

Sam had to be flown into Burlington under a cloak of secrecy in order to attend the conference. Since his conversion to Christianity from Islam, a fatwa has been placed on his life – a lifelong death threat required by the laws of the Quran. Sam is a formidable authority on Islamic issues and has special expertise on Sharia law. Formerly an Imam and from a Middle Eastern country, he was raised to become an authority on everything pertaining to Islamic religious and political law. Though not a big man, he spoke with a booming voice. It was easy to imagine that voice travelling throughout the district of his Middle Eastern home, broadcast from a towering minaret in one of the mosques where he regularly preached.

Sam, however, did not appear at the conference as a defender of Islam. He recited chilling passages of the Quran in powerful crescendos of Arabic and then translated those passages into English. He spoke in great detail of what it was like to live under Islamic Sharia law. I was mesmerized as I listened to his vivid description of what life under Islam was really like. All of the dreadful things I had come to learn about the religion that had settled so powerfully in my mind now struck a deep chord in my heart.

When Sam explained that he believed the greatest power of the Anti-Christ to visit the earth was and will forever be Islam, you could have heard a pin drop in the room. Sam also made it clear that Islam cannot ever be defined as a religion in the Western sense of the word, neither can it be termed as a faith only, for Islam is an all encompassing system and includes all branches of religious, social, political, legislative, judicial, and most of all, military life. Sam explained that Islam is founded on two primary and unquestioned authorities: the Quran and Sunah, which are the teachings and practices of Islam. Furthermore, what many Westerners do not understand is the centrality of the Mosque in Islam. The Mosque is considered by the West as a place of worship much like a church or temple. It is certainly a place where worship and prayer takes place. But most of all it is the centre of everything else Muslim.

Mosques are the epicenter of Muslim theology and the overseers of principles of Jihad. If a fatwa or death sentence is ordered it is issued from a Mosque.

Sam also emphasized how important it is for the West to understand the principle of *Takiyya*, which I learned about in my research and discuss in *Veiled Threat*. *Takiyya* permits Muslims to pretend to blend in with Western values until they can achieve and enforce a domination of Muslim values upon the culture in which they posture. It allows for the suspension of nearly all Islamic religious requirements when deemed necessary, and uses the language of Western beliefs and values so that Muslims appear in agreement with belief systems contrary to their own, even as they infiltrate it in order to ultimately dominate the belief system.

Sam illustrated just how at war Muslim values are with Western ideals of freedom of religion and freedom speech, when he invited a friend to the stage. His friend had difficulty walking and had to be led to the podium by the hand. The man bravely stood before us. The right side of his face was brutally scarred, almost beyond recognition. The eye above the vicious scars had been gouged out by his Muslim neighbors. Once his friends, when they learned he had converted to Christianity and became a follower of Christ, they inflicted the violence. In a furious act of justice, the neighbors attacked him with a broken Coke bottle and forever left grotesque marks in his flesh – a sign of his commitment and belief in a God of mercy and the very real cost of abandoning another.

I will never forget the image of this man as he spoke matter-of-factly in soft Arabic, without a hint of hate or anger in his words. In the moment I admit I did not share his sentiment. The words at the end of Psalm 139 that often make me uncomfortable suddenly made perfect sense as the poured out into my soul with quiet rage:

If only you would slay the wicked O God! Do I not hate those who hate you O Lord, and abhor those who rise up against you? I have nothing but hatred for them; I count them my enemies. Search me O God and know my heart, test me and know my anxious thoughts. See if there is any offensive way in me, and lead me in the way everlasting.

And yet the gospel of Jesus Christ makes me aware that these evildoers are still human beings firmly held in Satan's powerful grasp. The gospel of John tells us that, *"God did not send His Son into the world to condemn the world, but to save the world through Him"* (3:17). However, we cannot stop with this part of the scripture. For, the remaining verses complete the paradox and help us understand the unbelievable gift God offers mankind through His Son Jesus Christ, which can be just as easily accepted as it can be refused:

Whoever believes in Him is not condemned, but whoever does not believe stands condemned already because he has not believed in the name of God's one and only Son. This is the verdict: Light has come into the world, but men loved darkness instead of light because their deeds were evil. Everyone who does evil hates the light, and will not come into the light for fear that his deeds will be exposed. But whoever lives by the truth comes into the light, so that it may be seen plainly that what he has done has been done through God (18-21).

I believe I cannot, in my own wisdom, fully hold the two-sided sword of eternal truth in my hand, the truth that God will both utterly save and utterly destroy. Once we accept God's plan of unconditional forgiveness we fully recognize that it was nothing we deserved or earned. So in the fog of spiritual warfare those people who stand on both sides – those on the side of God's mercy and others on the side of judgment – fail to recognize the finality of the salvation story. Every human being, Muslims included, needs and can receive salvation. But Jesus and Islam will never be reconciled to each other: you are either with Christ or with Allah, you cannot side with both. Failing to understand that very basic concept will lead to many failed attempts at reaching out and reconciling with Muslims.

As I listened to Sam a deeper realization settled upon me as he highlighted that Muslim values cannot be reconciled to Western values, especially to the Christian faith. What became so frightening to me, and frustrating, was to realize how committed we are in the West to do these very things: go out of our way to convince ourselves that Islam is a religion of peace and that it can live comfortably at home alongside or within free and open democratic societies.

As a result of attending the conference in Ontario, and because of recent current events that have come to my attention at home and abroad, I found it necessary to write two additional chapters to include in the second edition of this book. The threat of Islam remains veiled, perhaps more than ever, in our oversensitive and politically correct culture.

And so it is with a few more words, extended research, and the inclusion of a few more personal experiences since I first published *Veiled Threat*, that I mean to once again sound the alarm and emphasize that if anything, the threat to our way of life is greater now than it was before.

- WK
Palm Springs, 2009

Chapter One: A World at War

The Believers fight in Allah's cause, they slay and are slain, kill and are killed

— *Quran 9:111*

WAKING TO EVIL

Recounting her own paradigm shift and the shift in the way her children viewed the world after the terrorist attacks in New York City, Nancy Gibbs, senior editor of *Time* wrote:

> We all have our favorite ways of measuring our kids. A pencil mark on the kitchen door. The pants that get suddenly too short. The favorite book they can finally read for themselves. But September 11 introduced a new system of measurement into our house: a yardstick marked off in innocence and discovery and recognition, of what the world contained.

> I discovered this where moms discover everything that matters in their children's lives: in the car. My daughters were in the backseat, one who had just turned four three days before the attacks, and her big six-almost-seven-year-old sister. The radio was on, even the giddy music stations were confused, do we escape into a more peaceful time, shanananana doo-wop, or interrupt with the latest update from downtown: the most recent body count; a funeral for a fireman; a message from the mayor. And the just-turned-four-year-old little sister listened to the news reports and shook her head, and waxed indignant, and said, "they should have been more careful. They should have watched where they were going, the men driving the airplanes. They shouldn't have hit the buildings. They should have been more careful."

And her big sister corrected her, as big sisters do, and in the process showed me the yardstick. "They were watching where they were going," she said. "They wanted to hit the buildings. It wasn't an accident." [1]

Gibbs continues, describing a moment in her children's lives that marked her as a parent, what she describes as an inevitable moment when children discover a world not "designed just to delight them; a world that has twists and caves and wounds laced through it, where evil has room to grow." Gibbs concludes that 11 September "tore down so many of the comfortable structures we've lived in for so long" but also gave parents new tools to "explain the heroism of soldiers and the stern sorrow of war and the price people through history have paid to achieve peace." [2]

Gibbs describes how her daughters awakened to the reality of evil in the world, and that though it can go unnoticed, evil ultimately rears its terrible head. When it does it reveals a world at war: a fight of values, between good and evil forces in a world where courage and despair are possibilities.

Somehow many people are forgetful or choose not to accept the reality of such a world. Like the four year old daughter whose mind was awakened to the reality of evil in the world, so must we all come to terms with the reality of evil. Imagine you have tickets to a play for the most acclaimed Broadway theatre production of your time. You made the trip to New York just to see it. The tickets were expensive, you purchased an elegant gown or rented a tuxedo, and you sit in the theatre, waiting for the show to begin. The air is electric with excitement as the curtains pull back. You close your eyes and sigh in delight, but when you open them, you are no longer in your seat: somehow you have been transported onto the stage instead! Your evening gown or tuxedo has disappeared and you are in full costume. You look out beyond the bright stage lights to the first few rows of faces in the audience, they calmly smile and wait for you to deliver your lines and begin the play. Although you do not know how it happened, you have been thrown into the middle of the drama as an actor but have no idea what to do. Your mind is blank, you are confused, and everyone else on stage and in the audience is looking at you to take your cue. Suddenly you have a good idea, you shut your eyes tightly hoping that when you open them again the terrible nightmare will have faded and you will be in your seat again. Your heart stops in your chest as you slowly open your eyes to floodlights, nervous actors, and a disappointed audience.

Our lives are like this imagined scenario. Many are only just waking up to the truth: we all have a part to play in an on-going story. History, our stage, is not something rehearsed or imagined on a Broadway stage. We have all been thrown into the middle of a greater drama that goes beyond us and began before us, a story that involves real good and real evil, and a part for all to play. Although it is difficult, even terrifying for some to face the truth, if we are all players in the drama, an appropriate question is, *what are we supposed to do and how will it all play out?*

The Bible describes a spiritual battle that began before mankind was created. Somewhere between, "In the Beginning" and the creation of our first parents, an enormous and eternity-changing event took place, described in scripture simply with the following sentence: "And there was war in heaven"[3] between Michael the archangel, leader of the army of God and Satan and his angles.

Scripture gives very few details about how or when Satan fell. But we clearly understand from scripture that Satan is the enemy of God and humankind, an accuser, murderer, and liar who seeks to destroy humanity and undermine God's work.[4] Many writers, thinkers, and theologians have and still do grapple with the mystery of Satan's fall. Few have imagined it as vividly as John Milton in *Paradise Lost.*

Milton imagines Satan make his way through the fury of the warring angelic armies to face the great archangel Michael, who, at the head of the faithful servants of God, smites entire rebelling angel squadrons in the single swipe of his sword. There on the field of battle the mighty captains meet. Michael turns and confronts the traitor, hardly able to believe the malice of Satan to disturb the peace of heaven and turn once upright and faithful beings into creatures suddenly made false. Milton imagines that the moment when Michael faces Satan to cast him from heaven was:

> Unspeakable…for like gods they seemed,
> Stood they or moved, in stature, motion, arms
> Fit to decide the empire of great heav'n.
> Now waved their fiery swords, and in the air
> Made horrid circles; two broad suns their shields
> Blazed opposite, while expectation stood
> In horror… one stroke they aimed…but the sword
> Of Michael from the armoury of God
> Was given him tempered so, that neither keen
> Nor solid might resist that edge: it met
> The sword of Satan with deep force to smite
> Descending, in half cut sheer; nor stayed,
> But, with swift wheel reverse, deep entering, [sheared]
> All his right side; then Satan first knew pain.[5]

Fantastic and lyrical, Milton's vision of Satan's fall from heaven might not be an historical account of the origin of evil, but it does highlight that when humankind's story began, it began against the backdrop of a very real war.

Yet, many people seem to live life not believing in an on-going spiritual battle between forces of good and evil, nor do they seem to recognize that humans are involved in the fight. Why have so many people forgotten such a basic truth and lived for so long ignoring historical facts such as the struggle between good and evil? Why is it that it takes atrocious acts like the terrorist attacks in New York, or the more recent bombings in Madrid and London for people to wake up momentarily to understand a greater war is being waged and that humanity is caught centre stage in the middle of the action?

John Eldridge explains that many of our favourite stories are great epics in which a hero must overcome great obstacles and eventually defeat an evil villain, often sacrificially. Recent films such as the new *Star Wars* or *Lord of the Rings* trilogies, *Braveheart*, *Gladiator*, *The Matrix*, and others are such epics. Whether stories are fairy tales or myths, Westerns or science fiction fantasies, the protagonists that we love face great evil and great risk, and in the process become incredible heroes.[6]

Though interesting, how familiar villains such as Darth Vader, Sauron, or Agent Smith arrived in the narratives they belong to is not as important as the fact that they are the evil enemies good characters must avoid, resist and fight. In the same way Satan, of whom all fictional villains are echoes and shadows, must be resisted in the real life story we live during our time on earth. That our favourite stories have similar plot elements and themes that depend on sacrifice, heroism, and very real conflict between good and evil is no coincidence but points to the often forgotten or disdained reality of the overarching cosmic drama. A fact, which Eldridge suggests, makes life an exciting if not risky adventure; something "dangerous now unfolding," leaving us with the responsibility to discover the "crucial role" we have been given to play.[7]

The Backdrop of our War

In an uncertain world it seems that one thing is certain: we as humans do not agree on much. What might seem very clear to one person is a mystery to the next. Whether we discuss political views, religious belief, theories about the origins of things, it does not take much time to realize that profound questions are not answered in a chorus of genuine agreement. The hotly contested United States Presidential elections in 2000, Canada's recent decision in Parliament to pass bill C-38 to legalize same sex marriages, the war in Iraq: when we discuss current events, as a society we are often bitterly divided on many issues. Often such conversations only end in outright disgust and bitterness; people feel very strongly about their opinions and there is great polarization. Reality is much more complex than left and right, Liberal and Conservative, them and us. There are myriad voices and opinions. However, it seems that The United States, Canada, and many other countries in the Western world are divided between two dominant political persuasions and moral opinions; both sides seem to fight for the mind share of the culture. Conservatives cry foul that a strong left wing voice assumes to interpret and speak for the conscience of society while Liberals are outraged by any hint of 'fundamental' values expressed in the press or social institutions.

Although the status quo seems to be characterized by disunity, political polarization, and disagreement, North Americans have demonstrated sustained moments of unity when they can forget political loyalties and stand side by side, united in a cause. Recent tragedies such as Hurricane Katrina, terrorist bombings in London, the 2004 Tsunami in South East Asia, and the Madrid bombings united North Americans in grief. What followed was an outpouring of unmatched compassion and generosity as people forgot political loyalties suddenly made insignificant and realized the undeniable value of human life. 9/11, that ill-fated day, was perhaps a day when North Americans stood together most united. In the face of unimaginable terror and devastation, Liberals and Conservatives, the left and right, had a revelation: there is another enemy. 9/11 changed our world, or, perhaps opened our eyes to a world that had already changed.

Humans have an inherent capacity to forget. Sadly, the revelation of the greater enemy is fading into forgetfulness; too many of us have closed our eyes again to the shocking truth and picked up the weapons of rhetoric and politically correct dialogue, while that enemy plots and conspires to strike again. History screams lessons at us, and yet our ears do not hear. If we are to avoid the devastations of the past, we must make every effort to remember and put into practice things our ancestors learned. We simply cannot afford to learn only from the mistakes we make in our day. Wisdom says we must learn from the mistakes of others as well, so that we do not repeat them, so we can save ourselves from unnecessary pain and heartache.

One lesson we have learned from history is that we as nations need discernment about when we should go to war and why we should fight. A recent documentary, "Canada and the New American Empire,"[8] examines the relationship between the two countries, once great allies. Irreverently, the documentary refers to The United States as the American Empire, a statement that gives a false impression of the past. Empires fought wars for merely selfish and political reasons. The Great War, World War I, began after the assassination of Arch Duke Franz Ferdinand. The Arch Duke's death was simply the fuse that ignited the war, the switch that turned because of tremendous senses of nationalism, unprecedented military mobilization, and political alliances. Europe had become a powder keg waiting to explode, obliterating several million young men in its stead. If ever there was reason not to send millions of men to war, it was World War I. Brave men fought and gave their lives simply out of duty to the leaders of their Empires, but not for much else.

However, some wars, like World War II, must be fought as brave men and women resist great evils that cannot be tolerated but can only be overcome with force. I was born in Holland in 1941, the first year of the country's occupation by the Germans. Most of my memories from the Second World War come from family stories told to me after the fighting was over, but I do have a few very clear memories of my own.

I recall Nazi officers at the door of our two story brick townhouse, looking for my father who was part of the Dutch Underground. My father was hiding under my parents' bed. If found, he would have faced immediate execution. I was not more than four years old, but I will never forget the urgent fear in the house at the possibility that my father might be discovered by the Nazis. Hoping to spend time with his young family, a four year old boy and two younger daughters that he missed during long periods of hiding, my father risked a trip to the house. I cannot imagine my mother's fear: our family's future hinged on whether or not the Nazis walked in the door to look for him.

By some miracle, my dad's younger brother was at the house that day. He had surprised us earlier with some meagre rations of food. Dad's brother was able to stop the two Nazi soldiers at the front door and somehow convince them there was no need to search our home. Years later I was told that there was a secret trap door in our home where someone could hide. In the sudden frenzy marked by the Nazi officers' unexpected visit to the house, Dad was unable to reach the hiding place in time.

I also recall the jubilation we felt as the war ended. I remember standing in front of our upstairs window as Allied planes dropped bundles of life-saving rations. The last year of the war was very harsh and many Dutch citizens died of starvation.

Although the above memories are firmly fixed in my mind, others are not as clear. Even though the sound of an air siren gives me chills to this day, I do not recall the many times air-raid sirens went off and I took my younger sister by the hand and sat with her at the bottom of the stairs as we waited for the Allied planes to fly over on their bombing raids from Britain to Germany. Nor do I have any memory of the evening when an anti-aircraft shell came through our roof and landed in my bed. My mother, for some reason, felt that she needed to take me out of my room; a short time later the shrapnel tore through our roof and landed where I slept. These stories I know only because they were told to me later in life, after the war.

My clearest memory, one I hold fast to, is of the sacrifice so many Canadian soldiers paid for the freedom of a very young boy, his family and countrymen, in a foreign land far across the ocean, virtual strangers. The Canadian soldiers belonged to a greater coalition of Allies who fought against the evils of Hitler's Third Reich. Every year after the war we placed flowers on the graves of Canadian soldiers. Our gesture was a small, insignificant sign of gratitude, but it was heartfelt and deeply personal.

Young men, boys just out of their teens, not much older than I, died far away from their homes. The ultimate price they paid, laying down their lives and promising futures, has always been difficult for me to come to terms with. And yet without the sacrifice, the world would have seen the Third Reich reign as a world power for generations to come.

The sacrifice of so many lives is hard to accept, even more difficult to be thankful for, and yet it prevented further horror and evil in the world. Ideally, we all hope such sacrifices will not be required of us in the present or the future; we also hope to never be confronted with evils and horror similar to Hitler's Third Reich. To avoid the need for such sacrifice and to prevent such evil, we proclaim the mantra, "Never again!"

We are now aware that if certain pre-World War II signs and warnings had been listened to and acted upon, the final price of suffering and the amount of lives lost would not have been nearly as horrendous. And yet I fear, even as we say and mean "Never again!" that the lessons of the past have not truly been taken to heart, nor are they applied to new dangers we face today.

As a matter of fact, even as I write these words large demonstrations in America, Britain and several Western countries have been staged, calling for an end to what many call an unjust war in Iraq. Angry crowds are seen on our television screens marching and wildly calling President George Bush and Britain's Tony Blair evil warmongers.

One voice in the angry crowd is Jean Hudon, coordinator of the Earth Rainbow Network whose mandate is to see the dream of peace, love, and harmony on earth "come true." She writes that "since the Bush administration has concocted it's fake terrorist attack on Sept. 11, 2001 as an excuse to launch it's program of wars of conquest infamously named the 'War on Terror' a growing number of governments bent on keeping their hold onto power have walked in the US footsteps and have been increasingly resorting to torture to terrorize their populations into submission."[9]

Hudon announces peace when there is no peace, imagining a world with no war and naming the wrong enemy. Conspiracy theories that Bush or Blair schemed the War on Terror as a ploy to wield greater power seems as ridiculous as a prevalent belief throughout the Muslim world that the 9/11 attacks were staged, planned and carried out by Israel, insane arguments in light of other facts: millions of Muslims in Islamic countries danced in the streets when they saw the World Trade Center destroyed by suicide pilots; two men leading their countries in a war on terrorism risking political futures and extreme unpopularity.

Has history forgotten that the same was said of Winston Churchill in the early 1930s? At the time, Churchill was scorned and mocked by his own party and countrymen. He was called a warmonger by some, while others questioned his sanity. Today his speeches are remembered as speeches of unequalled eloquence and courage. There was a time, however, when the same speeches were considered by most as the rants of a fool.

There are a number of signs for us at present, one we saw in the sky on that horrible day in September, and will forever be seared in our memories. Following the terrorist attacks of 9/11 were bombings in Madrid and London, memories that still shock and horrify us. Andrew Sullivan, senior editor at the *New Republic*, writes that the terrorist attacks in The United States:

> showed us that we stand deeply vulnerable to a destructive force in some ways more dangerous than even the last two totalitarian powers Americans were called to defeat. This enemy refuses to fight with honour; it hides and disappears and re-emerges whenever its purposes are served; it may soon have access to weapons that Hitler and Stalin only dreamt of. But it cannot be defeated the way Nazi Germany and Communist Russia were defeated because it is more like a virus than a host, infecting and capturing nation states, like Afghanistan, and then moving on to others. So we will have to act to pre-empt it this time, in Iraq and elsewhere, or it will be too late to resist it at all. For Sept. 11 showed us that, for the first time in history, the American homeland is actually vulnerable to a deadly foreign enemy. Only those in deep denial can forget that.[10]

According to Sullivan, the terrorist attacks are both warning and wake up call to citizens of The United States, an event that, despite all appearances of normalcy soon achieved in the "business as usual" mandate after the 9/11 attacks, changed the country. Liberals in Canada and The United States are severely critical of the war, and rightly lament the loss of young soldiers' lives. Cindy Sheehan the mother of a soldier who died in Iraq and who, in protest of the war, camped out at George W. Bush's Texas Ranch demanding an audience with the President, has become a spokesperson, even a pawn, in the Liberal movement that wishes to end the war and bring the soldiers home. In the heated debate about the Bush administration's agenda in fighting the war, important facts have been forgotten. We rightly desire that no soldiers lose lives, but we forget that whether or not we fight, there will still be a war. Sullivan concludes that:

> The illusion of isolationism has been ripped apart. How can America opt out of the world when the world refuses to leave America alone? The illusion of appeasement has been destroyed. Do we really think that by coddling regimes like Iraq or Syria or Iran or Saudi Arabia, we will help defuse the evil that lurks in their societies? The illusion of American exceptionalism has been shattered. The whole dream of this continent – that it was a place where you could safely leave the old world and its resentments behind – was ended that day. A whole generation will grow up with this as its most formative experience – a whole younger generation that knows that there actually is a right and a wrong, and that neutrality is no longer an option. That generational power has only

just begun to transform the culture. In decades time we will look back and see what a difference it made.[11]

The terrorist attacks in The United States revealed to us an enemy we had not seen or understood. The attacks in Madrid and London confirmed they are here to stay. I believe The United States must not only understand this accomplished and determined enemy, but must face it as well, and so must every other country that calls itself free and democratic.

Today, we find ourselves in a completely different world. Wars are fought on buses and trains, subways and in skyscrapers. Soldiers of this war live in our own neighbourhoods and secretly plan atrocious attacks against unsuspecting people. The purpose of this book, then, is to bring a clear awareness of the danger that has appeared in these new times. I believe that the new war is a war of spiritual agendas played out in the "real world" including the political arena, a fact that is misunderstood in our times and certainly unrecognized in a secular and politically correct Western society.

It is this grave misunderstanding, that there is an ongoing spiritual battle between good and evil, that must be understood before we are able to act in a unified way against the great evil that grips our world today. In the pages that follow I hope my findings will bring truth to the minds of people faced with a struggle that will define our times. We must face the reality that we are at war, a war I pray we, like the brave Allied soldiers who fought in World War II, will fight with courage to protect the lives and freedom we so dearly value, so that when we look back in decades' time, it will be with thankfulness and not regret.

If we have been born against the backdrop of an ongoing spiritual war, it follows that all people fight on a side. Those who have not yet opened their eyes to this reality may passively fight on one side of the battle, but fight nonetheless. All people, all over the globe, are involved in the war. The war has many battlefronts and many modes of fighting. I wish to consider one front of the war.

Many people would identify one of the greatest threats to peace and security in the world today as the militant and fanatical *jihad* or holy war of extremist Muslims who have hijacked an otherwise peaceful religion. Their terrorist acts have pock-marked our world. These so-called misguided fanatics can be found in Iraq, Iran, Pakistan, Afghanistan, and Saudi Arabia to name a few states. Increasingly, however, they turn up within our own countries and neighborhoods.

Perhaps the most astonishing and unbelievable part of our new war is that such terrorists have used the democratic freedom afforded to them in the Western world to try to institute a new reign of terror. And, while the Western world tries to align itself against the threat to its freedom, it ignores important facts.

Muslim terrorists have declared that the war they wage is a religious war; they have announced that their struggle is between good and evil. The war on terrorism is more than a political struggle, and in the West we must come to terms with the fact that the battle involves religion and faith. We must understand our enemy.

My main concern is to wake the sleeping masses to the reality of the real roots of terrorism. Until we eliminate the immense hurdle of political correctness and begin to understand the difference between what Muslims believe and what we think or are told they believe, we will continue to head toward great danger and disaster.

Islam is in our world to stay. The threat of terrorism and holy war will characterize our times as never before, therefore to understand the theological foundation of Islam and what Allah, the Quran, and Muhammad actually demand of all believers and non-believers is essential. I believe that the heart of the Muslim religion is bad; its practices are rooted in a history of militant and violent tribalism that continues to loot and bring destruction to the world. Islam, as a religion, must have a change of heart if it is to coexist with the rest of the world as many Muslims and non-Muslims desire. If it does not, we will be forced, even against our will, to sharpen our swords.

CHAPTER TWO: THE ROOTS OF ISLAM

the natural mystic does know that there is some-
thing there; something behind the clouds or within
the trees

> – *G.K. Chesterton in Everlasting Man*

People of the Camel

To begin our journey toward understanding the war we find ourselves in, we must go back in time 1400 years to a desolate and harsh desert in Arabia. In the sixth century, the economic conditions of desert-dwelling Arabs improved significantly because of the lavish city of Constantinople. With its expensive tastes, Constantinople imported a steady stream of Oriental goods. Courtiers of the great city dressed in Chinese silk, churches and cathedrals required huge quantities of incense and other Oriental materials, food now required rare spices, people developed a nose for rare perfumes. Exotic cloth, precious stones, pepper and other products came from India. These luxurious goods were brought by sea to South Arabian ports, then by caravan northward to Constantinople. The import of Oriental goods created the biggest economic boom the Arabian Peninsula had ever seen, and in turn thrust the once insignificant Arabs onto the stage of world affairs. These Arabs, known in English as "Bedouins" or "desert-dwellers" were not a nation, but had a clan system, and shared similar traditions and values.

Bedouins of the twenty-first century do not differ much from Bedouins of the sixth century who depended on what the desert provided, as well as their flocks of sheep, goats, and camels for survival. Sixth century Bedouin tents were partitioned: a section was given to the women and children and another was given for the family head to entertain his male guests. Rapid mobility was essential; all tools and utensils fit into boxes and could be loaded along with the tents on camels when necessary.

Each tent in a Bedouin camp represented a family unit. Several family units formed a clan, and the clan constituted every Bedouin society. The clan provided every Bedouin his means of livelihood; it represented his law and government; it served as his school, private club, the executor of his estate. Each clan chose its own chief who made treaties on the clan's behalf, ransomed members made prisoner, and settled internal disputes. He cared for the clan's poor and could claim one-fourth of all spoils from the *razzia*, that is, raids on rival clans. Clans increased wealth and population through such raids, acquiring goods, women, and slaves.

From its desert origins, Arabic emerged as a language rich in subtlety and graduations in meaning. Its lilting cadences made it a superb medium for lyrical verse. Ancient Bedouin poetry was preserved solely by recitation and revels in war, in the thrill of stalking an unsuspecting enemy, bursting upon him to steal his livestock, women and children, and then vanishing without trace into the trackless sands. Besides being a great warrior, a great man was also an accomplished orator and a lavish host.

Bedouin nomads needed the products of towns, and acquired them either by raiding and stealing, or by exchanging property for protection. Every clan was at constant risk of a raid by another clan. If he did not lie awake worrying about who might attack him, a Bedouin man lay scheming about who he might attack. *Razzia*, the name given to this tribal status quo of robbing and raiding other clans, has been described by some as the Arab's "chronic mental condition."[1] Strabo, a geographer in the first century BC noted that "every Arab is a tradesman and a robber." Other men gave them names, but the name these Arabs gave themselves was "The People of the Camel," men willing to steal, fight, and die for the survival of their clan.

THE PROPHET AND A DESERT CREATURE

The People of the Camel worshipped the sun, moon and nature. Their ultimate realities were birth, marriage, food, rain, death, goats, sheep, camels, and travel.[2] In the sixth century AD, on one of his journeys to Mecca for an annual celebration, Adbel Muttalib a desert-dwelling nomad, made a vow to his desert god: "Grant me sons and I promise to sacrifice my tenth son to you." Years passed and Adbel was blessed with many children, always knowing that a future son would have to be sacrificed to appease his god.

The tenth son, Abdullah, was born and grew into a young boy who was much loved by his father Adbel and all his sisters. The family pleaded that Abdel not honour the vow he made to the god, and eventually Adbel approached the Kaba in Mecca, a place where pilgrims enacted various forms of worship, and bargained with the gods. Adbel, wanting to save Abdullah, bartered with the god and offered to sacrifice ten camels in exchange for the life of his beloved son. The god was not pleased, so Adbel continued to cast lots until they revealed a favourable response: one hundred camels in exchange for his son's life.[3]

MUHAMMAD

Adbel's interaction with his desert deity was no small matter. His willingness to sacrifice the life of a child in exchange for family and wealth, followed by his desperation to save that child when faced with the consequence of the bargain he made, thrust him deeply into the spiritual domain and created a precedent through which his descendants would encounter and serve his god.

Around AD 570 Abdullah, about twenty-five years old, married a young woman named Aminah. Six months into their marriage, Abdullah joined a caravan headed for Syria where he hoped to make his fortune. On the journey, Abdullah caught a fever and died, leaving behind his pregnant wife and a son he would never know. When the young widow presented the baby to her father-in-law, the old man carried him to the Kaba and named him Muhammad, a rarely heard name until that time meaning "greatly praised."[4] Aminah was too poor to care for her young son, so her father-in-law arranged for nomadic herders to care for the child for the first five years of his life. By the time he was ten years old, Muhammad was orphaned three times. When he was returned to his mother at five years old, Aminah soon became ill and died. After his mother's death, he was given into the care of his grandfather, then into the care of his uncle Abu Talib after his grandfather's death.

Muhammad grew up as a poor shepherd, tending sheep, but at the age of twenty-five, like his father before him, was given an opportunity to lead a caravan of camels to Syria. The wealthy widow who hired him fell in love with Muhammad and asked him to marry her. Although Khadijah was forty years old, Muhammad loved her and they were married. Khadijah and Muhammad had four daughters; their two sons died in infancy.

After fifteen years of marriage, Muhammad became restless and began to retreat to a lonely mountain cave to meditate and search for answers to the mysteries of life. It was in this cave where events took place that would forever change the history of our world. Suddenly, Muhammad began to have spiritual experiences. Desert Arabs believed in the existence of Jinns, spiritual beings both good and evil in origin. In the cave, Muhammad met a powerful creature from the unseen world who told Muhammad: "I am Gabriel and you are the messenger from Allah".[5] The encounter with the spirit deeply effected Muhammad: he ran from the cave in great fear at the encounter, and when he reached home, begged his wife to cover and hide him from the terrible being.

While her husband shivered feverishly in fear through the night, Khadijah went to consult her Christian cousin about her husband's experience. The old, blind cousin, when told what happened, concluded that if Muhammad's story was really true, then the angel who spoke to him had to be the same angel who spoke to Moses.

After consulting her cousin, Khadijah listened to her terrified husband recount that the creature told him to warn his people to call them back to the service of Allah. "But whom shall I call, and who will listen?" Muhammad asked his wife. "I will listen," she replied, and the world had its first convert to Islam,[6] a religion that has over a billion followers around the globe.

CHAPTER THREE:
POWER BEHIND THE SWORD OF ISLAM

Know that paradise is under the shade of swords

— Muhammad[1]

A Pagan Face Lift

How did a new religion that now captivates one out of five people on earth begin in such an austere and desolate place? Clearly, more-than-human power was at work. Even before Muhammad was born, his grandfather Abdel set a precedent for spiritual powers to negotiate and interact with his bloodline and set the stage, preparing the way for Muhammad's ministry in the world.

Such statements, that there are spiritual powers at work, are unpopular in the Western world and are cynically, even sarcastically, received. We can, however, clearly conclude that spiritual powers are at work not only in our times, but also have been throughout human history. The great evil of Nazism in recent history serves as an example that evil spiritual forces are at work in the world.

By the end of World War I, Germany was in a desperate position, relegated to pay the unbearable burden of war reparation debts. Proud and industrious, the Germanic people alleviated some of their suffering by revisiting shared stories from the past that were founded in pagan culture. Athletic and gymnastic clubs began to train the youth culture to develop a vigorous physical lifestyle. After training sessions old stories were told to remind young minds of mythic Germanic warriors that once ruled supreme.

The old war gods Wodin, Thor, and the ultimate god Valhalla inspired young men to dream of great conquest once again. From these myths grew the concept of the Pure Aryan race, a master race that could justify the extermination of any race inferior to itself. Eventually human breeding projects resulted. Pairing mates of "acceptable" bloodlines was allowed, as was the extermination of humans deemed inferior, horrors and evil remembered as some of, if not the worst crimes against humanity.

Unimaginably atrocious and heinous acts were carried out, promoted by Germans of high standing. An SS officer could, after a most delightful lunch, end the lives of a dozen captured Jews with a pistol shot to each of the victims' heads then sit down in the evening to a nice dinner in the presence of friends and chosen guests, accompanied by wonderful chamber music. Men of high culture were capable of such debase acts.

We agree that the horrors of the Third Reich were inhuman. The Nazi party began with a spiritual and political agenda of evil adopted by a few that eventually ruled an entire nation then tried to rule the world. How many people at that time expected that one group unified around an ideology of hatred, superiority, and fear would eventually lead to the death of 50 million people? Thankfully the great evil of the Third Reich was overcome, but only at a great and terrible price. Is it not possible that such evil can take other forms, and appear differently elsewhere in history?

Islam, like Nazism, had roots in pagan rituals. If demonic powers could influence the world to set the stage for the supreme destruction of World War II in a supposedly civilized part of the Western World, could not such powers achieve similar horror through the stark barbarism of the desert Arab environment?

The psychological condition of life in the desert, *razzia*, raiding and warring to survive, was deeply engrained in Muhammad and became deeply engrained in Muhammad's religion as well. For example, soon after his cave revelations, Muhammad had a small group of loyal followers. The band raided and grew in wealth; Muhammad, throughout his life had ten wives and various concubines most procured by ambush and slaughter. Muhammad would become a great chief among the Arabs, a warrior and orator who to this day can summon men to fight in the name of Allah to cleanse the world of Infidel. From history, we see that the driving force behind Islam is the power of the sword. A weapon and a symbol that has maintained its authority for the past 1400 years.

CONFLICTS THAT SHAPED THE SPIRITUAL
LANDSCAPE OF THE DESERT

Many say that Judaism, Christianity, and Islam, the world's three monotheistic religions, are more similar than dissimilar: branches from the same root. Though Islam has similar practices to Judaism, which likely exist as a result of their connection by blood,[2] it is important to note that Islam as a religion grew out of Arab paganism in the way that Christianity grew out of Judaism.

The pre-Islamic faith of the People of the Camel clearly was centred on real spiritual power. Islam and early desert Arab paganism might not be one and the same, however the Muslim faith has striking similarities to pre-Islamic Arab pagan practices, and maintains pagan Arab's holy sight, diety, and various rituals.

> The first and most important doctrine in the creed of
> Islam is the doctrine of Allah. Muhammad knew from
> childhood the native pre-Islamic belief in Alilah, mean-
> ing 'the god,' a vague high God who created the world
> and became Allah or God.[3]

Although there are genetic and some spiritual similarities between Judaism, Christianity, and Islam, history clearly shows that the three religions are and do remain distinct from each other. Islam was born and developed into a full-fledged faith throughout the sixth century[4] and the first signs of conflict between it and Christianity seem to be rooted in disputes over pagan practices.

Around the time of Muhammad's birth, somewhere near the year AD 570, the Christian ruler of Yemen launched an offensive against Mecca. His soldiers ordered the town to surrender. The soldiers meant no harm against the people, but wanted to destroy the box-like structure called the Kaba which, according to Arab legend, was an altar built by Abraham at the place where his exiled handmaiden Hagar and her son Ishmael discovered a spring of water.[5] The object drew thousands of Arab pilgrims to Mecca each year, a pilgrimage that resulted in degenerate sexual rites as a part of the pagan worship of the desert moon god Alilah and his three sisters, Lat, Uzza, and Manat, who were occasionally offered human sacrifices.[6] The Meccan's refused to comply with the Yemen ruler's request. Legend tells that the pagan Arabs prayed to their god that the Cross would not triumph over the Kaba and their prayers were effective, unleashing a great evil power against the soldiers. According to Arab folklore, the desert god Alilah listened, and the Christian forces woke in the morning with small pox; in disorder they fled back to Yemen.

In the pre-Islamic world, Christians also had conflict with Jews in sixth century Arabia. After the destruction of Jerusalem nearly five hundred years earlier in AD 70, surviving Jews were scattered all over the Roman Empire, and several Jewish tribes were established in Arabia. By the fifth century they had established numerous communities. Christians had also established some roots in the area but were outnumbered by the Jews. The two faiths, at times, were mutually hostile towards each other; the Christian claim that Christ was the Jewish Messiah was a point of contention that, historically, has caused significant conflict between Christians and Jews.[7]

The Jewish ruler around the year 523 had an Arabic nickname, "Dhu Nuwas," which meant "Curlylocks." Dhu Nuwas was evil and treacherous. He opposed an order of Christians in Narjan, the Sons and Daughters of the Covenant, known for their zeal for Christ, who were undertaking efforts to produce an Arabic Bible. When Dhu Nuwas attacked Narjan, he was likely unaware of the city's zeal: children were taught from their early years of understanding that they must, if need be, die for their faith.

When he sent three army units to defeat the city, Hadith, the commander of the Najranites, met the invaders on the battlefield and defeated all three units. The Jewish king laid siege to the city but could not penetrate its defences. Baffled, he finally sent an emissary with an offer of peace. If the city surrendered, he would swear on the Torah that the Christians would suffer no physical harm. Furthermore, the Christians would be allowed to practice their faith. Hadith adamantly opposed the offer of peace, but he was talked into the agreement, assured a Jew would not break such a hallowed oath. Hadith's decision to agree to peace was a fatal mistake. Dhu Nuwas had no intention of keeping his oath, he executed every Christian not prepared to renounce his faith and embrace Judaism. Not one man complied, and all were herded into the city's biggest church. The church was set on fire and not one man survived.

Women and children were also rounded up and told that if they would spit on the Cross, denounce Christ, and embrace Judaism their lives would be spared. None complied and soldiers were told to herd all the women and children into a tight group. Archers sent hails of arrows in their midst until all were killed. Ruhayma, the wife of Hadith, as well as his daughters and granddaughters, had been spared because Ruhayma besides being a beautiful, saintly woman revered by Christians and Jews for her kindness and generosity, had once loaned money to Dhu Nuwas' father, then forgiven the debt. Ruhayma was arrested with the other women, but then released. The Jewish king sent word to her that if she recanted her religion and embraced Judaism, her personal fortune would be preserved. She would also be permitted to marry a high official of his realm. Ruhayma publicly appealed to those Christian women who still lived to follow her example, and spat in the Jewish king's face. She was beheaded, as were her daughters and granddaughters.[8]

The ruling powers of Constantinople heard about the barbaric treachery of Dhu Nuwas and launched a counter offensive from Ethiopia. Syrian documents record that Dhu Nuwas was captured by Ethiopians who took him in a boat, tied heavy pots around his neck, and dumped him overboard. With Dhu Nuwas perished the last Jewish State in the Middle East until the founding of Israel more than 1400 years later. An "army" of Christian faithful who lived not by violence also perished, giving their lives to preach and teach to the People of the Camel.

EVIL TRIUMPHS OVER GOOD

We, in the West, are not familiar with a lifestyle of warfare; we live in unprecedented times of peace, different from most any other time in world history. Surely the sixth century was a different time. In an environment where Christians had come to give their lives in an effort to bring the good news of the Gospel to the People of the Camel, the stage had been cleared for Muhammad's new religion to succeed as Jewish and Christian populations were reduced.

Muhammad garnered support for his new-found faith slowly as friends and family accepted that he was Allah's prophet. His first convert was his wife, followed by his cousin Ali and then a house slave. Later, Muhammad's friend Abu Bakr became a follower. By AD 620 Muhammad was offered protection from powerful families north of Mecca, protection he needed from various Meccan clans that vowed to assassinate him, a plot that Muhammad learned of from the creature who spoke to him in the cave who called itself Gabriel.

Responding to the threat, Muhammad and his small band of converts fled to Medina, a city where Muhammad carried out increasingly barbaric raids. Medina proved to be an excellent base for attack and retreat. Muhammad re-stigmatised the raids as holy missions performed for Allah. Warriors could have sex with women in the tribes they raided and kill without hesitation; if the warriors perished, the rewards of paradise awaited them. If they survived, they prospered.

Life in the desert was volatile, a battle of clans and faiths for survival. However, it was not impossible for two different faiths to make alliances. Soon after Muhammad began to interact with the creature in the cave, he counted on the support of the Medina Jews who were a minority in the city. Muhammad's treaty with the Jews guaranteed them continued use of their synagogues and in return the Jews promised their support in the event of war.

In AD 627 an army numbering 10,000 soldiers was sent by Mecca to Medina to eradicate Muhammad, and yet, astonishingly, the soldiers were defeated by Muhammad, his 3000 men, and the support of the residents of Medina.

For a time, sixth century Jews were politically aligned with Muhammad and his growing band of converts. But the Jews soon learned that treaties could not always be trusted. As the conversations with the creature that called itself Gabriel continued, Muhammad's alliance to and opinion of Jews began to change as his theology evolved and developed. Furthermore, Muhammad began to experience opposition from Jews, which quickly became a problem. Scripture, well known to the Jews, often clearly contradicted the teachings of Muhammad. The Medina Jews often heckled Muhammad during his sermons, perhaps ridiculing him for claiming that Ishmael was the child Abraham took to Mount Moriah when the patriarch was tested by God, or, that Muhammad had ongoing conversations with Gabriel, the same angel with whom Moses spoke.[9] Allah's prophet, Muhammad, was often unable to answer the Jew's difficult questions.

The growing disparity between the Jews and Muhammad had dangerous implications and Jewish opposition to Muhammad proved to be a dilemma for Allah's prophet: Muhammad had previously recognized the Jews as the original people of God. Suddenly, God's people were contradicting and embarrassing God's prophet. The differences between the Jews and Muhammad and his group of followers grew increasingly clear. At some point, Muhammad demanded that the Medina Jews recognise him as the prophet of God. They refused. As a result an incident was soon invented: a Jewish boy was accused of lifting the skirts of a Muslim girl. The offended kinsman of the girl killed the accused boy which caused an uproar in the Jewish community. Jews responded by killing the Muslim kinsman in retaliation.[10]

The conspiracy to further polarize Jews and Muhammad worked. The Jews' act of retaliation provided Muhammad and his followers with a reason to openly despise the Jews. By AD 625, the conflict between Jews and Muhammad had escalated. After the army from Mecca was defeated in AD 627, Muhammad and his men announced that the Jews in Medina collaborated with the Meccans and confrontation of a more violent nature occurred between Muhammad's forces and the Jews. Muhammad invaded Jewish settlements and violated old laws previously held in common between Muhammadans and Jews. For instance, Muhammad told his men to uproot the Jewish tribe's date palms, an act forbidden by the law of Moses. Muhammad tweaked the rule to serve his purposes: claiming it was the will of Allah, the prophet revealed that, suddenly, Muslims enjoyed special exemption from the rule.[11]

Advised by the angel Gabriel, the time came to deal with the Banu Qurayza, Medina's last Jews. Muhammad did so with an act of butchery that would permanently poison Islamic-Jewish relations. The Qurayza were barricaded within their fortress about three miles southeast of the city. As Muhammad's army approached the stronghold, flights of Jewish arrows rained hard upon them. One Muslim ventured to the fortress walls, and was killed by a huge millstone pushed upon him from above by a Jewess. But the Qurayza sensed they were doomed.

The Medina Jews had three difficult choices before them, which their leader outlined. Firstly, they could embrace Islam and thereby betray God. Second, they could kill their wives and children to keep them from Muhammad's advancing army, and then fight to the death. Thirdly, they could attack on a Saturday, catching the Muslims off guard, but violate God's Sabbath law as a result. The people rejected all three options and appealed instead to the Aws, an Arab tribe, who on a previous occasion they had saved from destruction. The advice of the Aws chief was clear: to surrender was to perish; they should fight Muhammad's army to the death.

After giving the above advice to the Medina Jews, the Aws chief rushed back to his people, guilt-stricken. He had betrayed the prophet, he said, by telling the Qurayza the truth. Was not war supposed to be deceit? As penance for his truthfulness, the Aws chief, ordered his daughter to tie him to a post in the mosque, where for some fifteen days he remained until Muhammad, informed by Gabriel that he had suffered enough, ordered him to free himself. The spot is still known as the "Pillar of Repentance."

Ultimately, the Qurayza did surrender twenty-five days later, on the condition that their fate be determined by the Aws chief whom they trusted. Muhammad agreed. But the decision, in the end, was not made by their former friend. Instead of deciding the fate of the Jews on his own, the Aws chief, perhaps aware of his tendency to betray the prophet, called upon the grand chief of the Aws federation, a merciless man who deeply despised the Jews. This dignitary, a grossly corpulent man, physically supported by his aids, was transported to the Qurayza fort. While his kinsman pleaded with him to spare their allies, the Muslim army envisioned vast booty within the fortress, and eyed the Jewish women. Muhammad himself had set his eye on one particular prize, the beautiful teenager Rheihana.

"Proceed with your judgement," ordered the prophet. "My judgement," said the fat Aws chieftain, "is that the men be put to death, the women and children sold into slavery, and the spoil divided amongst the army." Wails of agony were silenced by a wave of Muhammad's hand. The chief's decision, he pronounced, was "the judgement of God".[12]

All the male Jews were dragged into Medina and penned in an enclosure, where they prayed through the night, exhorting each other to remain steadfast in their faith. Muhammad, they reasoned, could not possibly behead some 800 men. Muhammad, tragically, betrayed the Jews' hope in an act of monstrous cruelty. Pretending to promote an orderly peace settlement, Muhammad had the 800 Jewish men come to confirm what he called a "peace arrangement" in groups of six. But, rather than confirm peace, Muhammad forced all 800 Jews, six at a time, to kneel, and then executed them. All 800 men were beheaded, their bodies thrown into a deep trench dug by his men the night before. The small groups and the lie about peace was a ploy to prevent panic or a possible Jewish retaliation. The deceit also ensured that Muhammad and his men accumulated a lot of wealth.

The booty was, indeed, large: fifteen hundred swords, a thousand lances, five hundred shields and three hundred coats of mail, flocks of sheep and camels, gold and silver vessels, jewels and beautiful household furnishings, and about a thousand women. Muhammad took one-fifth of the war prize and the remaining four-fifths went to his army. The wives and children of the men were divided among Muhammad and his men as slaves and concubines.[13] Among the women Muhammad took was Reihana. The prophet proposed marriage as soon as Reihana's husband, brothers and father had been executed, yet she refused to wed him and died in his harem four years later.

About the slaughter of the entire male population of the Medina Jews, American Muslim writer Yahiya Emerick, explains the facts differently:

> After a hard fought battle, the Banu Quraiza agreed to surrender on the condition that their fate be judged by the chief of Aws tribe, with whom they had good relations. After the Banu Quraiza warriors were taken into custody, the Aws chief asked the clan leaders what their punishment should be for betrayal according to the Torah. And of course the (800) warriors were executed by the verdict of their own religion. The women, children, and non-combatants remained unharmed.[14]

By AD 628, Muhammad's final solution to the Jewish problem was realized in Khaybar, where with just sixteen hundred men, he systematically attacked seven different Jewish fortresses and eliminated ten thousand Jewish men.

BEYOND MUHAMMAD: TRANSITIONS IN LEADERSHIP

In late May of the year AD 632 Muhammad became ill. The cause was not certain: some scholars say it was pleurisy that afflicted him, others say he was poisoned. Whatever the cause, Allah's prophet was very ill; Muhammad died on 8 June 632. The events following Muhammad's death recall the recent intrigue that followed the death of Yasar Arafat, former leader of the Palestinian Liberation Organisation (PLO) in 2004. As soon as Muhammad died, immense grief and confusion took over the camps of his followers; mourners crowded his death site wailing in lament. In the hysteria and grief of the moment Umar, one of Muhammad's early converts and a leading warrior among his ranks of men, approached the body. In a fit of desperate emotion he shouted, "The prophet is not dead! He has only swooned away!"[15]

Confusion resulted. Some followers tried to convince Umar that he was wrong and that the prophet had really died. Umar thundered back "You lie! The prophet will not die until he has rooted out every hypocrite and unbeliever."

In the midst of the madness, certain decisions were made. Abu Bakr, Muhammad's friend and an original convert, was chosen as Muhammad's successor on the same day that Muhammad died.[16] Internal battles ensued. A self proclaimed prophet and Muhammad imitator, named Tulaiha, was eliminated under the leadership of King Khalid and his four thousand warriors. Other impostors and power seekers were killed and bloody battles were waged between desert Arab tribes, who fought each other for the leadership of Islam.

By mid 633 Muslims had defeated all the apostasy throughout Arabia. Once united, Muslim clans waged wars and won victories throughout the region. The military strategy of the desert warriors was primitive and successful: rob, rape, slaughter, and run before Imperial troops were sent to defend the cities under attack. The tools of their trade were well supported by worthy animals. Camels could out-manoeuvre opponent armies. On camels, the Arabs could attack quickly and then retreat, easily escaping over the soft desert sand because of their unique feet. As well, the desert Arab's horses had developed through the harsh centuries a greater lung capacity with their enlarged nostrils. These two superior mounts gave the fearless Muslim warriors a decisive advantage in their bloody attacks.

CHAPTER FOUR:
THE SWORD AND THE CROSS

*We have a prophet by whom we will conquer
all men*

— *(Ishaq 471)*

THE SPREAD OF ISLAM

The failure of Christianity to capture the hearts of desert dwelling Arabs has been a difficult problem for Christian theologians to solve. Some point out the serious theological conflicts of the faith in a pagan world, and cite that the doctrine of the Trinity was misunderstood and rejected. Others note that Christianity was confined mostly to cosmopolitan cities where Christians were merely one of many resident peoples. The elimination of Jewish tribes and the Najran Christians certainly played a part as well. [1]

In a world immersed in social and spiritual change, desert Arabs found it difficult to embrace the gospel of peace within their *razzia* paradigm. Even as Arabia for all intents and purposes looked like the new frontier for Christianity, the faith encountered a great spiritual force:

> For the first six centuries, the Christian story is one of strife and struggle rewarded by undeniable success. The cross, the symbol of an ignominious death by execution, had by the year 600 risen triumphantly above churches from Ireland in the Atlantic to the shores of the Indian Ocean. Jesus' assurance that the gospel would be preached to all peoples seemed a prophecy in the course of imminent fulfillment. But then, from a direction no one expected, disaster struck Christendom. Within barely a century, more than half of the peoples who had at least nominally declared themselves Christian were lost to a new faith through military conquest – undeniably the greatest reversal Christianity would be called upon to suffer in its first two thousand years. The name of the conqueror was Islam. [2]

Early on Muhammad's writing suggested his new religion was tolerant in nature. Modern day scholars note that the Quran emphasized compassion but as Muhammad experienced resistance in Mecca and was forced to flee to Medina and protect himself, the Quran's message of compassion turned to a message of retribution.[3] While Muhammad and his few original followers lived in Mecca, they were a minority group surrounded by enemies. At the time, likely because of the circumstances, Muhammad's message was more conciliatory, and the prophet portrayed himself as a simple messenger:

> There is no compulsion in religion. The right direction is henceforth distinct from error. And he who rejects false deities and believeth in Allah hath grasped a firm handhold which will never break. Allah is Hearer, Knower.[4]

Once his political power was established, Muhammad's armies went forth to attack surrounding tribes, or other nations. They offered three options: accept Islam, pay tribute, or die by the sword:

> Fight those from among the People of the Book (Jews and Christians) who believe not in Allah, nor in the Last Day, nor hold as unlawful that which Allah and His messenger have declared to be unlawful nor follow the true religion, and who have not yet made peace with you, until they pay the tax willingly and make their submission.[5]

Dr. Anis A. Shorrosh, an Arab Christian asks the question: "What would you and your family choose?" and cites that numerous Christians, when faced with the Muslim ultimatum, paid with their lives. "Yet the numbers of those who took the easy way out were far greater. As a result, many church buildings were turned into mosques to please the conquering Muslims, and a shroud of spiritual darkness covered huge areas of the Middle East, North Africa and Spain."[6] As recently as the beginning of the twentieth century, around one million Armenian Christians were savagely slaughtered by Turkish Muslims. Since Muhammad raised his sword in the desert, Islam has demanded, "Convert or die; Bend to Allah's will and change, or, pay the price."

ISLAM REWRITES CHRISTIAN HISTORY

As the sword of Islam fell upon Arabia in battle, another mighty sword, the pen, was used in the religion's quest for power. Muhammad, in the name of Allah, waged ideological war against the Christian faith, even rewriting its history, announcing the Christian faith was suddenly obsolete.

In his book *Understanding Islam*, Yahiya Emerick, a historian and Muslim scholar explains that the Quran, Allah's message to the world, reached humanity through a chain of communication: Allah spoke to the angel Gabriel, Gabriel spoke a message given in pieces to Muhammad over a period of 23 years, and Muhammad shared that message with the world. When Muhammad was 63 years, the revelation was complete, and the prophet became Allah's final messenger to humanity, "and therefore the Quran is the last message which Allah has sent [humanity]. Its predecessors such as the Torah, Psalms and Gospels have all been superseded."[7]

The Quran teaches that Jesus was a secondary prophet who was rescued by God from death at the hand of Jewish leaders who named him an impostor, arrested him, and meant to kill him. The Quran states that Jesus was not executed, even if it appeared that he was; in the confusion of the moment, Romans executed the wrong man, Jesus' betrayer, an easy mistake to make for Caucasians distributing justice in a region where "all Semites look the same."[8]

That an illiterate man could be instrumental in a complete rewrite of hundreds of years of carefully documented and preserved Christian history is alarming. Although illiterate and one man, Muhammad announced that thousands of years of Biblical history, recorded over the centuries by forty literate writers whose accounts are verified by thousands of witnesses, was suddenly obsolete. He made such a grand statement, and Muslims like Emerick still do today, though the different books of the Bible consistently predict the same fulfilled prophecies, expound on the same themes, and were preserved by countless scholars in thousands of meticulously recorded, separate manuscripts.

An example of Islam's adaptation of Jewish and Christian history occurs in the story of Zechariah the Jewish priest as told in the Quran:

> Zachariah prayed to his Lord: Lord, grant me from Thyself pure offspring, surely thou art the Hearer of prayer. The angels called to him as he stood praying in the chamber: Allah gives thee glad tidings of Yahya, who shall fulfil a word of Allah; he will be noble, chaste and a prophet from among the righteous. Zachariah submitted: Lord, how shall I have a youth as my son when I am already of advanced age and moreover my wife is barren. He responded: Such is the power of Allah, He does what he pleases. Zachariah beseeched: My Lord, lay upon me a special commandment. He replied: The commandment for thee is that thou shalt not communicate with people for three days except by signs, and shalt remember thy Lord much and shalt glorify Him night and morn.[9]

In the original Jewish account, the story of Zechariah's encounter told throughout all the hill country of Judea,[10] recorded also in the Bible, differs significantly:

> In the days of Herod, the king of Judea, there was a certain priest named Zacharias, of the course of Abijah. And his wife was of the daughters of Aaron, and her name was Elizabeth. And they were both righteous before God, walking blameless in all the commandments and ordinances of the Lord. And they had no child, because Elizabeth was barren. And both were advanced in their days. And it happened in his serving in the order of his course, before God, according to the custom of the priests, it was his lot to burn incense when he went into the temple of the Lord. And all the multitude of the people were praying outside at the time of incense. And an angel of the Lord appeared to him as he was standing on the right of the altar of incense. And seeing this, Zacharias was troubled, and fear fell on him. But the angel said to him, Do not fear, Zacharias. For your prayer is heard, and your wife Elizabeth shall bear you a son, and you shall call his name John. And you shall have joy and gladness, and many shall rejoice at his birth. For he shall be great in the sight of the Lord, and shall neither drink wine nor strong drink. And he shall be filled with the Holy Spirit, even from his mother's womb. And he shall turn many of the sons of Israel to the Lord their God. And he shall go before Him in the spirit and power of Elijah, to turn the hearts of the fathers to the children, and the disobedient to the wisdom of the just, to make ready a people prepared for the Lord. And Zacharias said to the angel, By what shall

I know this? For I am old, and my wife is advanced in her days. And answering, the angel said to him, I am Gabriel, who stands before God. And I am sent to speak to you and to show you these glad tidings. And behold, you shall be silent and not able to speak until the day that these things shall be performed, because you did not believe my words which shall be fulfilled in their time.

And the people waited for Zacharias and marveled that he stayed so long in the temple. And when he came out, he could not speak to them. And they perceived that he had seen a vision in the temple. And he was making signs to them, and remained speechless.[11]

The difference between the texts is striking. Muhammad, the recipient and author of the Quran, claims the angel Gabriel recounted to him the story of Zechariah and the miracle birth of his son. The Bible tells the story differently and claims the angel Gabriel, who appears briefly to only two other individuals at decisive moments in recorded Judeo-Christian history,[12] was a key character in the narrative itself. Either the Quran or the Bible has the wrong angel.

Zechariah was either mute for three days as a sign to him of the power of Allah, or he was mute for nine months because of his unbelief. Gabriel either prepared Muhammad as God's final prophet to the world in the sixth century, or announced the birth of a child who would prepare the first century, then the world, for a Saviour. Gabriel was either in the desert cave with Muhammad recounting Zechariah's story or he was in the temple with Zechariah, but the contradictory accounts reveal he could not have visited both locations.

Surely the authors' approaches to recording the respective narratives might explain the difference: Muhammad told the story after a series of revelations from a frightening creature he encountered in a dark cave; Luke, the Greek physician, recorded his account after careful investigation and consultation with eyewitnesses and Biblical scholars.[13]

Christianity and Islam differ in other ways as well. Christ encourages his followers to ask questions as they to seek to discover truth, the revelation of which Jesus assures will always set people free.[14] Muhammad forbids it: Questioning Islam and the Quran is not allowed.[15] Strangely enough, lying is permitted and even encouraged for the sake of Allah by the theological concept of Taqiyya. Muslims were granted this right to infiltrate non-believers. The intent of Taqiyya is to deceive unbelievers about Islam for the explicit purpose of putting to rest doubts and questions about the religion.

Muhammad set the precedent of this deceptive tradition in the sixth century when he called for the assassination of a local poet, K'ab bin Ashraf, who ridiculed him. The poet's step-brother volunteered and asked Muhammad if he could lie to Ashraf in order to lure him out of his fortress to kill him. Muhammad permitted him to lie, a decision that lined up with the teaching of the Quran: *Kill (disbelievers) wherever you find them... Be in wait for them at every place of ambush and lure them with lies or the truth.*[16] As one Imam says, "Speaking is a means to achieve objectives. Praiseworthy aims are attained through both telling the truth and lying."[17]

Muhammad himself bent laws and standards he himself imposed when it suited his purposes, something Christ never did. After a successful battle against Jews, an especially beautiful Jew widowed in the battle caught Muhammad's eye. At a victory banquet that evening Safiyah, the widow, was presented to Muhammad as part of the plunder, and the prophet consummated his marriage to her that very night. The consummation violated a rule Muhammad imposed on his followers: no man could sleep with his new wife until she had completed her menstrual cycle so that paternity of children could be ensured.[18] On another occasion, Muhammad took for himself a six-year old bride named A'isha, after a conquest. He consummated the marriage with the girl when she was nine.[19]

Where Muhammad changed laws that were inconvenient for him to follow, Christ kept the spirit of the law, freeing people from unnecessary human rules that kept people in bondage. The founders of Islam and Christianity differ as clearly as their comparative passages of scripture. But where Christianity and Islam differ most significantly is on what they say about the nature of God himself.

CHRIST AND MUHAMMAD

In the first century AD, Christ claimed not only to be a prophetic messenger from God, but God himself. Christ gave a face to the name of the God of the Old Testament, a God of mercy and compassion who is slow to anger but who judges those who do not receive his mercy.[20] In his book which considers world history as it is informed by the Incarnation, G.K. Chesterton concludes that Christ sets himself apart from all other religious leaders with his claim of divinity:

> Mahomedans did not misunderstand Mahomet and sup-
> pose he was Allah. Jews did not misinterpret Moses and
> identify him as Jehovah. Why was this claim alone exag-
> gerated unless this alone was made? Even if Christianity
> was one vast universal blunder, it is still a blunder as
> solitary as the Incarnation.[21]

Chesterton asserts that Jesus' ministry differs from the ministries of other prophets and philosophies because his was a journey with an object.

Like a mythic hero in search of treasure, the gold Christ sought was his own death; the primary thing he came to do on earth was to die.[22] It is here that Islam and Christianity most differ. Christ asks his followers to "love your enemies and do good to them,"[23] believing God will judge between good and evil; Muhammad tells his followers to wait in ambush for the enemy and when they least expect it, to slaughter them. Where Christ healed the sick and fed the hungry, Muhammad raped, murdered, enslaved, and destroyed his enemies' food supply. Muhammad raises the sword to the world; Christ offered his life and was raised on a cross. Muhammad converts or kills the infidel, Christ allowed the infidel to kill him. The emphatic difference between the Muslim and Christian faiths is the very difference between their final prophets and their Gods. Islam is sustained by the power of the sword; Christianity is sustained by the power of the cross. With the belief that the Gospel of peace and the power of selfless sacrifice are obsolete, Muhammad and present day Muslims, in the name of their God, continue to change the world.

CHAPTER FIVE: THE POWER OF ONE

But even if we, or an angel from heaven, preach any other gospel to you than what we have preached to you, let him be accursed.

— The Apostle Paul to the Galatians

Either the Christian faith is absolutely true or Islam is the absolute truth based on the claims of the religions' prophets. I believe that when Christianity and Islam are compared and fairly evaluated the above statement is the only conclusion that can be made. Although I now utter the statement, I admit the conclusion came to me as a surprise when I began my research. I now see that the two faiths worship different Gods and are expressions of opposite spiritual kingdoms. The Muslim religion has been the enemy of Christendom for the past 1400 years. I believe that one is a false religion and evil; the other is true and good.

Although I think Islam is wicked at the heart, I recognize that there are Muslims who are good, kind, compassionate, and who honestly seek God, wanting peace. At the same time, there are people who claim to be Christians that are not good people and who could learn character qualities from Muslims. Reality is complex. So are faith and the human heart. I believe in a merciful God who knows the hearts of humankind. Islam and Christianity, however, as well as their holy writings, are as far apart as heaven and hell. The following three reasons are why I identify that the heart of Islam is bad.

REVELATION

There is no doubt that a real and profound spiritual experience took place in the life of Muhammad. The creature that met with Muhammad in the cave was simply demonic. Spiritual evil exists. For Muhammad, his contact with evil was predetermined by his grandfather's agreement with the desert god at the Kaba.

The profoundly illogical and human failure of Islam, as in the case of other evil religions and cults, is that there were no witnesses to verify the divine revelation and information that their founders relay. Muhammad's testimony and the subsequent holy book is one man's story: a story now believed by one out of every five people on the face of the earth. Surely the spiritual force behind the religion, the creature in the cave, is powerful.

In the New Testament we read about Satan's very real power in the world.

> *Then Jesus was led up by the Spirit into the wilderness to be tempted by the devil. He fasted forty days and forty nights, and afterwards he was famished. The tempter came and said to him, 'If you are the Son of God, command these stones to become loaves of bread.' But he answered, 'It is written: "One does not live by bread alone, but by every word that comes from the mouth of God."'*

> *Then the devil took him to the pinnacle of the temple, saying to him, 'If you are the Son of God, throw yourself down; for it was written, "He will command his angels concerning you," and "On their hands they will bear you up, so that you will not dash your foot against a stone."' Jesus said to him, 'Again it is written, "Do not put the Lord your God to the test."'*

> *Again, the devil took him to a very high mountain and showed him all the kingdoms of the world and their splendour; and he said to him, 'All these I will give you, if you will fall down and worship me.' Jesus said to him, 'Away with you, Satan! for it is written, "Worship the Lord your God, and serve only him."' Then the devil left him, and suddenly angels came and waited on him.* [1]

The above account reveals Satan had very real authority on earth to grant influence and power. And here we come to an interesting point. When alone in the wilderness, Christ had a spiritual experience with a creature, and when he heard its words, he relied on the previous and familiar words of God as recorded by revered and criticized scholars. Muhammad, when he had a spiritual encounter in the wilderness, rewrote those scriptures, even calling them irrelevant, then went on to clutch and grab at the power so many men desire and are tempted by: wealth, riches, influence.

FOUNDATION

The foundation on which Christianity is based can and has been explained in endless volumes of doctrine and apologetics. The search for truth in the Christian faith is so overwhelming and profoundly convincing that it promises the true seeker of Truth will never be disappointed. The Bible contains the God-inspired writings of 40 authors, with hundreds of its prophecies fulfilled by events recorded in world history, more than forty which were fulfilled in the historical man, Jesus Christ. Furthermore, every revelation that involved Jesus Christ was witnessed in all cases by several eye-witnesses.

Islam cannot make such a claim, nor can its prophet Muhammad. The Quran is the product of the private experiences and revelations of a single man. Many of the expositions in Islam's holy book cannot be considered "inspired". The Quran simply cannot be trusted because it contains many contradictions. Even Muslims note the Quran is "profoundly at war with itself," full of a "bundle of contradictions" and "blatant inconsistencies." [2]

The greatest of these is called the "Prerogative of Abrogation." This legal term refers to the power to destruct or annul a former law:

Whatever previous commandment We abrogate or cause to be forgotten, We reveal in this Quran one better or the like thereof: Knowest thou not that Allah has full power to do all that he wills?[3]

The passage, while making Allah look and sound powerful, also makes him seem fickle and his sacred writings inconsistent: Allah can change his mind and will when a former law no longer "works." Muhammad's abrogation of laws which previously forbade men to have sex with the captured wives of defeated enemies until after their period, or his abrogation of laws which previously forbade soldiers to destroy the enemy's vineyards, are examples of what this theological provision looks like lived out. While it perhaps releases Muslims at convenient times into greater personal freedom, it seems a dangerous, self-serving doctrine at least, and seems to invalidate other passages of the Quran. The theological concept shows that, unlike Christian scripture which does not destroy former laws but fulfils them suggesting something solid and fixed, the Quran is unstable, a smorgasbord of tastes that could change at any time. Walter Martin highlights some of the problems and instability the Prerogative of Abrogation creates, with the following questions:

1. The Quran cannot be trusted because it contains "divinely inspired" contradictions. If God has a history of abrogating his own revelation, how can we be sure of his future intentions?
2. If Muhammad was the last prophet, what is keeping [Allah] from changing his mind and sending more prophets?
3. If God can change his word how can we ever be sure of our eternal destiny?
4. Since [Allah] can change his mind, he is either not all-knowing or he is a liar.

5. If [Allah] is not consistent, then his creatures have no foundation for morality or ethics.[4]

LOCATION

The woman said to [Jesus], 'Sir I perceive that you are a prophet. Our fathers worshipped in this mountain, and you people say that Jerusalem is the place where men ought to worship.'

Jesus said to her, 'Woman, believe Me, an hour is coming when neither in this mountain, nor in Jerusalem, shall you worship the Father...But an hour is coming, and now is, when the true worshippers shall worship the Father in spirit and truth; for such people the Father seeks to be His worshipers. God is spirit, and those who worship Him must worship Him in spirit and truth.'[5]

Christ taught his followers that worship was not limited to time or place, but that God could be praised everywhere, a truth consistent with the words of Old Testament prophets. Among the demands Islam places on its followers in regards to worship, including prayer five times during the day, complete submission involves worship in three true locations: Medina, Jerusalem, and Mecca. The most interesting and perhaps the most absurd stipulation of Islam, is Jerusalem as a Muslim Holy site. If there is any doubt as to the Muslim will and resolve behind this stipulation, one need only refer to the Palestinian National Charter. The charter makes it clear that armed struggle is the only solution to regaining the spiritual domain called "the land of Palestine." Jerusalem is an undeniable portion of that struggle and "liquidation of the Jews" is without a doubt part of the solution.[6]

How did such a tenacious position take root? One of the most beautiful structures in the Old City of Jerusalem holds the secret: the gold-plated Dome of the Rock. The impressive structure was built at the location where Muhammad claimed to have ascended to heaven during a night journey. Yahiya Emerick recounts the Muhammad's experience:

> One morning, Muhammad emerged from a relative's house, in which he spent the night, and made a public announcement so dramatic that some new converts to Islam threatened to renounce their faith. Muhammad said that he had been taken to Jerusalem, and ascended from there to heaven, and then had returned to Mecca-all in the same night!

> How did Muhammad explain all of this? He said that after he had finished his late-night prayer, the angel Gabriel came to him accompanied by a fantastic horse-like creature called the Buraq, whose every stride took it to the furthest extent of its eyesight. Muhammad mounted the Buraq, and they reached Jerusalem in a few minutes. The spirits of the past prophets appeared, and Muhammad led them all in prayer. Then Muhammad remounted the Buraq and Gabriel ascended with him into the next realm and through seven layers of heaven."[7]

During the vision of the night, Muhammad claimed to encounter Moses, Abraham, and a "reddish man of medium height, with lank hair and many freckles on his face" who could only be Jesus himself, a description of Christ strikingly different than the Semite easily confused for another olive skinned Jew at his botched crucifixion attempt.[8]

Though many of the then two hundred adherents to Muhammad's religion worried that their leader had lost his mind, without hearing the story from Muhammad himself, his future successor, Abu Bakr, in response to concerned followers exclaimed, "By God, if Muhammad himself has said it than it must be true!"[9] Although passages of the Quran require the proof of more than one witness in order for a legal decision to stand, the historic claim of Islam that Jerusalem is its holy site is a stipulation Muslims hold to unswervingly though there were no witnesses present to verify Muhammad's original experience. Perhaps this should cause no surprise, for the rest of Islam and its beliefs hinge upon the absolute witness and testimony of one man and one man only, and that witness is radically believed by multitudes the world round.

CHAPTER SIX: CONTEMPORARY ISLAM

I have been made victorious with terror

— Bukhari , Allah's Apostle[1]

ANTI-SEMITISM

Iranian President Mahmoud Ahmadinejad's recent public statement that Israel should be, "wiped off the map" created an international uproar and was condemned by the United Nations Security Council.

> But the uproar has caused confusion in Iran, where such rhetoric has been commonplace since the 1979 Islamic revolution. Anti-Israeli diatribes are painted as murals along most highways and are heard regularly at Friday prayers. "Our respected president has not said anything new or unprecedented about Israel to justify such a huge political tumult," wrote Hossein Shariatmadari, who was appointed to his post as editor of the Kayhan daily by Iran's Supreme Leader. "Iran's nuclear case ... could be a reason for the recent clamor." [2]

These comments stunned many in the West with their blatant rhetoric of violence, hatred, and anti-Semitism. Perhaps what is more shocking is that Iranians attempt to brush off the comments as consistent with the state's government and in turn criticize the world for morally reprehensible behavior: concern about the state of Iran's nuclear weapons program. Shariatmadari reminds the West of Iran's consistent opinion of the Jewish state and highlights that the West is out of touch with reality.

Why are we shocked that powerful Muslims leading Muslim nations like Iran make such statements? We have not been careful students of the Quran. The traditional, orthodox Muslim position on Jews is recorded in some of the following passages of Islam's holy book:

Humiliation and wretchedness were stamped on the Jews and they were visited with Allah's wrath.

But you (Jews) went back on our word and were losers. So become apes, despised and hated. We made an example of you.

Sufficient for the Jew is the flaming fire.

Jews are people who will listen to any lie and Christians are enemies.

Fight those from among the People of the Book (Jews and Christians) who believe not in Allah.

We (Muslims) shall rouse our slaves to shame and ravage you (Jews) disfiguring your faces. They will enter the temple as before and destroy, laying waste to all they conquer.

Allah made the Jews leave their homes by terrorizing them so that you killed some.[3]

The Quran and it scholars teach a very real, very "stubborn"[4] anti-Semitism that should alarm us, an anti-Semitism that dates back to the time just after Muhammad's death. The Pact of Umar, the man who assumed leadership of the growing Muslim faith after his predecessors Abu and Muhammad, imposed rules on Christians and Jews that turned them into second class citizens. Christians and Jews were not allowed to travel on the middle of roads, could not sit in the marketplace, and were to stay out of the way of Muslims. They were required to differentiate themselves from horse-riding Muslims by strictly riding donkeys. What is more, foreshadowing the Nazi requirement of twentieth century Jews leading up to the Holocaust, Umar demanded that Christians and Jews distinguish themselves as such by putting a specific mark on their headgear.[5]

The idea that Jews and people of other faiths are different and less than Muslims pervades Islam. For example, a Muslim cleric was caught on tape saying, "Jews are offspring of apes and pigs," an allusion to a passage in the Quran:

> Say: 'People of the Book! Do you disapprove of us for no other reason than that we believe in Allah, and the revelation that has come to us and that which came before?' Say: 'Shall I point out to you something much worse than this by the treatment it received from Allah? Those who incurred the curse of Allah and His wrath, those of whom He transformed into apes and swine.[6]

When questioned about his racist statement, the cleric lied, saying, "Oh no! You misunderstood. I said Jews are the offspring of 'grapes' and 'figs.'"[7] Taqiyya, which literally means "concealing or disguising one's beliefs, convictions, ideas, feelings, opinions and strategies,"[8] can marry and co-exist nicely in Islam. In light of the known practice of Taqiyya, what then do we make of the statement by a Muslim academic attempting to explain Islam to the non-Muslim world: "Islam is a peaceful religion, Islam treats women as equals and Islam does not believe in killing those who are not believers"?[9]

Brigitte Gabriel, a journalist and news producer who started her career as an anchor for *World News*, an evening Arabic news broadcast throughout the Middle East, recalls the suffering her family and fellow Christians experienced during the Lebanese civil war, which, in hindsight she refers to as "the first front in the worldwide Jihad of militant Islam against the only Christian country in the Middle East."[10] During the war, her family's home was shelled and destroyed leaving Gabriel wounded, and forcing her to live underground in a bomb shelter from age 10 to 17, without electricity and very little food. Gabriel recalls crawling under sniper bullets to find water for her elderly parents.

While growing up in Lebanon, Gabriel was always told that Jews were the seed of Satan, a lie she believed until she and her mother arrived in a hospital in Israel and the care and compassion of Jews revealed the truth about Jews. Gabriel explains that the Lebanese war waged against 'Infidel' Christians, the 9/11 terrorist attacks, and anti-Semitism all come under the banner of a religious "bigotry and intolerance" that is advanced by Islam, a religion she says threatens states and indiscriminately thrusts people into its dangerous path: Jews, Christians, Arabs, Westerners, and Easterners alike.

In her childhood, Gabriel and many others suffered greatly under Yasar Arafat who, at the time, was lauded as a conscientious leader by the West. To his death, Arafat was courted by the West and its desire to see peace in the Middle East, even as his political adherents waged war against Israel and committed countless acts of terror. The striking disparity between the opinion of Arafat in the press and those who really suffered under his fanatical terrorism only highlights how seriously the real threat of radical Islam is overlooked, a threat some warn is a "new" anti-Semitism that spreads around the globe: "a dangerous worldwide coalition of Islamic terrorists, well-intended but profoundly misinformed students, right-wing fascists, left wing ideologues... and sensation-seeking international media"[11] who would more readily blame the Jewish state for the current world crisis, than cry foul at Islam.

We have not carefully considered Islam's track record throughout history. Most Westerners are shocked but silent about statements like the one made by Iran's president, then walk on egg shells, meek and mild, unwilling to state publicly that they question whether Islam truly is a peaceful religion. Few people voice their concerns blatantly, and when they do, they shock and offend our precious political correctness. Craig Winn is one such voice. Winn has received death threats for words like the ones below, the tagline of his book, *Prophet of Doom*:

> Islam is a caustic blend of regurgitated paganism and twisted Bible stories. Muhammad, its lone prophet, conceived this religion solely to satiate his lust for power, sex, and money. He was a terrorist. If you think these conclusions are shocking, wait until you see the evidence.[12]

The evidence Winn points to is recorded Islamic religious writings which confirm that Islam's prophet, far from being peaceful, was a thief, liar, assassin, involved in mass murder, who engaged in paedophilia, incest and rape.

Such comments cannot be made lightly. And it is not fair to paint all Muslims with the same brush. Surely millions of Muslims simply desire to have families and peacefully live their lives. If, however, we examine the facts about Islam in today's world, we see patterns of behaviour that match Winn's blatant statement, and suggest that there is something wrong with Islam at the heart.

VIOLENCE AND PERSECUTION

I admit astonishment at the positive press Islam receives today. Books like *Understanding Islam* assure us that Islam is a misunderstood religion and that it relates closely to Judaism and Christianity. Yet continued violence in the name of Allah is troubling. And, when compared to its

Judeo-Christian brother, Islam seems simply that, a relative by blood, but not in spirit. Islam must address the ugly facts of violence, oppression, and hatred that plague the religion if we in the West are to accept that the faith is peaceful and, in turn, try to co-exist with it.

Islam's violent past is disturbing:

> From the first historical example of the 800 beheaded Medinan Jews, to the more recent examples of 50,000 Greeks and Armenians massacred in 1822, the 10,000 Armenians and Nestorians murdered in 1850, 11,000 Maronites and Syrians in 1860, 15,000 Bulgarians in 1876, 10,000 Armenians in 1894, 325,000 from 1895 to 1908, 30,000 Armenians in 1909, and 80% of the Armenian population (1.5 million) wiped out in 1915 to 1918, religious persecution has been a frequent occurrence under Islam. In the 1980's and 1990's Muslim's in North Sudan were either starving or selling into slavery Black Christians and Animists in the south. Oppression against non-Muslims in general but Christians in particular has also occurred in Saudi Arabia, Pakistan, Libya, Muaritania, Nigeria, and Tanzania. In 1990 it was believed that Mauritania had at least 400,000 slaves. In 1990 Iran began a campaign of persecution against Christians, especially the Assemblies of God.[13]

In recent days, Christian parents in the Sudan have suffered the raid and destruction of their villages, slaughter of their cattle, enslavement of their children, brutal murder of family members, and are faced with an agonizing question: "Do I denounce Christianity in order to obtain food, medicine, and education for my starving children?" The tradition of violence that became part and parcel of Muhammad's religion was rooted in the way of life in sixth century Arabia and was passed on to subsequent leaders of the now global faith, a mandate to see the world fall to its knees in true Islam: *total submission.*

In Sudan it is estimated that the number of Sudanese who have died in submission to Islamic jihad since 1983 is 2.5 million people, more deaths than in Rawanda, Bosnia, Somalia, and Kosovo combined which are other areas scarred deeply by the sword of jihad; the holy mandate has left over one million persons displaced by the genocide living in shantytowns around Khartoum.[14] Fifty thousand children of the Dinka tribe alone are held as slaves. Omar Hassan al Turabi, leader of Sudan's Muslim Brotherhood, ordered that Christians be killed on sight, and takes pride in the fact that government soldiers kill, rape, and maim in the name of Allah.[15]

One of two fates awaits captured young Christian boys. They may be sold into slavery to Muslim families in Northern Sudan or Libya, where they will be given Muslim names, forced to renounce their Christian faith, say Muslim prayers, are whipped, and given little food. If they try to escape their Achilles tendons are often severed. Captured children that become too tired to walk have been known to be placed in burlap bags and thrown into rivers to drown. If a young boy is not sold into slavery, he is sent to Islamic re-education school where he will be forced to memorize the Quran in Arabic, renounce his religion, and participate in Islamic studies from early morning until late at night. A refusal to co-operate results in horrible beatings. Eventually, the young boy will be trained in the army to murder his own people.[16]

Young Christian girls face another kind of terrible fate. The Islamic Sudanese government has a policy of raping all women and girls who are abducted. One victim testifies about the horrors she endured from Sudanese Muslims:

Very early in the morning the enemy came and surrounded the whole village. They took 16 from just our family. The soldiers said, 'you will come with us to Mendi. If you refuse you will be killed.' On the way they said, 'something you have never seen before you will see at Mendi.' After dark, the soldiers came and took the girls to their rooms and raped them. I was taken and raped. When you have been taken the soldier will do what he wants, then he will go out of the room and another one will come in. It is continuous like this. Some are raped by four or five soldiers. If any cry in pain they are beaten. Every day the raping continued. It is impossible to count the men that raped me. It was continuous. Perhaps in a week I would have a day of rest. Sometimes a man would take me for the whole night. Sometimes I would be raped by four or five men. No women are spared; girls as young as 9 years old are raped. Mothers are molested repeatedly before the soldiers leave. Her breasts may be cut off because the soldiers know that then her baby will die of starvation. If they are young and pretty they will be sold to slave traders. Fathers of course are killed. Villages burned. Cattle are killed and all food supply destroyed. Churches are destroyed. Pastors and church members are often thrown into burning churches. Some pastors are crucified. [17]

In Sudan the government uses the Quran to justify a mandate of unthinkable cruelty and genocide, and announces it performs the will of Allah. Moderate Muslims also suffer under the regime for refusing to rape, torture, murder, and destroy, and so fulfil their duty to Allah and their government. *And there was war in heaven*, but it is fought here on earth.

Millions of Muslims have been brutalized by their religion's own evils so that, at a familial and societal level, they are left in poverty and hopelessness. This, also, is a fact that Islam must face. In her book *The Trouble with Islam*, Irshad Manji, a Muslim, argues that there are clear and troubling discrepancies and outright lies that the Islamic faith professes. Manji calls for change. She recounts her experiences growing up in a Muslim family that immigrated from West Africa to Canada. Her father ruled the family with a ready fist; Manji sums up his ideology of parenting:

> Don't laugh at dinner. When I steal your savings, shut up. When I kick your ass, remember; remember it will be harder the next time. When I pound your mother don't call the police. If they show up, I'll charm them into leaving, and you know they will. The moment they are gone, I'll slice off your ear. If you threaten to alert social services, I'll amputate your other ear.[18]

At home Manji was chased around the house by her knife-wielding father. Yet other events in her life like the ones that took place in her school or at the Rose of Sharon Baptist Church, helped Manji see another world outside the clutches of Islam: a world where fear and oppression were not mandatory.

OPPRESSION OF WOMEN

A reading of various passages in the Quran might make sense of the cruelty shown by some Muslim fathers like Manji's to their daughters.

> *Men are appointed as guardians over women, because of that in respect of which Allah has made some of them excel*

others, and because the men spend of their wealth. So virtuous women are obedient and safeguard, with Allah's help, matters the knowledge of which is shared by them with their husbands. Admonish those of them on whose part you apprehend disobedience, and leave them alone in their beds and beat them.[19]

As their guardians, men are entrusted with the responsibility of admonishing and disciplining women. It seems that some men have different standards for their wives and daughters. The ugly reality of "honour killings" in the Muslim countries has not been hidden from the world. A recent CBC documentary examined a case of honour killing in Afghanistan. A Muslim man became suspicious of his wife, believing she was unfaithful to him. Without investigation, merely on his suspicious hunch, the man shot his wife in the back with a shot-gun. For his crime, and in accordance with the second chapter of the Quran, the husband was asked to give one cow to the woman's family in return for their dead daughter's life. His freedom was celebrated in his village by other men who spoke of the man as a righteous Muslim, a true follower of Allah and his prophet. The dead woman's life was worth no more than a solitary farm animal.

Western influences outside of her Muslim upbringing compelled Manji to become educated rather than indoctrinated in what she calls the "tribal totalitarianism" that grips her religion and its followers and keeps them in a state of fear and superstition. Islam, Manji asserts, must address its oppression of women as second class members of the faith, reduced, eternally, to sexual objects for the male faithful.

Part of the suicide note Muhammad Atta, a leader among the terrorists in the 9/11 attacks, echoes the Quran and reads as follows:

Know that the gardens of paradise are waiting for [you martyrs] in all their beauty, and the women of Paradise are waiting for you in all their beauty, and the women of Paradise are waiting, calling out, come hither friend of God.[20]

Recruiters of Muslim terrorists dangle visions of seventy virgins in front of martyrdom candidates, Manji says, "like a perpetual license to ejaculate in exchange for a willingness to detonate."[21] The belief that 72 virgins await all Muslim martyrs along with Houri's, soulless women who satisfy all carnal desires, is a belief Manji highlights Islamic fanatics consider to be absolute truth. And it is likely a strong motivation for many to dress themselves in explosives, fulfil the will of Allah by killing the unbeliever, and so receive their eternal reward.

On the above point, French filmmaker Pierre Rehov agrees with Manji. Rehov's film *Suicide Killers* is based on interviews he conducted with the families of suicide bombers and would-be bombers in an attempt to find out why they enact terror. Through conversation with these Muslims, Rehov concludes:

> We are facing a neurosis at the level of an entire civiliza-
> tion. Most neuroses have in common a dramatic event,
> generally linked to an unacceptable sexual behavior. In
> this case, we are talking of kids living all their lives in
> pure frustration, with no opportunity to experience sex,
> love, tenderness or even understanding from the opposite
> sex. The separation between men and women in Islam is
> absolute. So is contempt toward women, who are totally
> dominated by men. This leads to a situation of pure
> anxiety, in which normal behavior is not possible. It is
> no coincidence that suicide killers are mostly young men
> dominated subconsciously by an overwhelming libido

that they not only cannot satisfy but are afraid of, as if it is the work of the devil. Since Islam describes heaven as a place where everything on Earth will finally be allowed, and promises 72 virgins to those frustrated kids, killing others and killing themselves to reach this redemption becomes their only solution.[22]

A Culture of Fear and Death

Perhaps the propensity for young Muslim men and some women to kill themselves and others for the faith is further explained by the Muslim understanding of the afterlife and passage into it. As Yahiya Emerick explains in *Understanding Islam*, a Muslim's standing before Allah will only be established after death when they are asked three questions by Munkir and Nakir, who Muhammad described as black-faced angels with blue eyes who wait for people at their death:

> *Who is your Lord, what was your way of life and who was your prophet?*

Correct responses afford the believer a comfortable resting place, the size of a coffin, where he or she waits the day of judgment; the Infidel who answer the questions incorrectly are stuffed in suffocating bins with a view of hell where they are tortured until the day of judgment. When that horrible day of judgment arrives, all humans will stand naked, waiting for their turn to be judged, a process that Muhammad writes could take as long as 50,000 years. Then, guilty or innocent, all must walk over the bridge that crosses the burning pit of hell where angels throw the worst sinners into the fire; even those Allah deems innocent, if not careful, risk falling into the terrible inferno. Good deeds on earth may help passage into paradise, or they may not. The death experience that Muslims anticipate is filled with fear. Surely the guarantee of Paradise through death by martyrdom is a much more desirable passage to the afterlife.

Rehov relays that speaking with families of martyrs was fascinating and terrifying, as he realized the people he spoke with "constantly battle against their own death anxiety." He concludes that "the only solution to this deep-seated pathology is to be willing to die and be rewarded in the afterlife in Paradise":

> You are dealing with seemingly normal people with very nice manners who have their own logic, which to a certain extent can make sense since they are so convinced that what they say is true. It is like dealing with pure craziness, like interviewing people in an asylum, since what they say, is for them, the absolute truth. I hear a mother saying "Thank God, my son is dead." Her son had became a *shaheed*, a martyr, which for her was a greater source of pride than if he had became an engineer, a doctor or a winner of the Nobel Prize. This system of values works completely backwards since their interpretation of Islam worships death much more than life. You are facing people whose only dream, only achievement goal is to fulfil what they believe to be their destiny, namely to be a *shaheed* or the family of a *shaheed*. They don't see the innocent being killed, they only see the impure that they have to destroy." [23]

To Rehov, the reality of suicide bombings exists for a number of reasons of which sexual repression, deception, and fear are at the forefront. But Rehov does not interpret the decision by Muslims to detonate as an end of repression and fear, but as a door into a better world: "They are seeking the reward that God has promised them. They work for God, the ultimate authority, above all human laws. They therefore experience this single delusional second of absolute power, where nothing bad can ever happen to them, since they become God's sword."[24]

Beyond suicide bombings, there are other ways that believers die for the Islamic faith. The story of Tina Isa, the sixteen year old daughter of Palestinian immigrants to St. Louis, Missouri shocked the United States. Although Tina's six other siblings "consistently adhered to the strict, traditional values of their Palestinian parents," Tina quickly adopted "the anything-but-traditional values of American adolescence." [25] Like her other siblings, Tina was forbidden to go on school trips, go to concerts, date, or visit friends on weekends, but she refused to abide by these prohibitions.

> Defying her parents, Tina took a job as a counter clerk at Wendy's fast-food restaurant and dated an African-American schoolmate. In so doing, she violated long-standing Arab understandings concerning appropriate behavior for young women and, in the eyes of her parents, brought shame and dishonor to the family name.[26]

On 7 November 1989, as she came home from a date with the boyfriend she dated against her parents' wishes, Tina's mother grabbed and held her while her father stabbed her to death: thirteen stabs in eight minutes. To the daughter's pleas for mercy her mother barked, "Shut-up!" and the father screamed over and over again, "Die my daughter, die! Die quickly my little one!"[27] The FBI discovered the truth behind the "honour killing" inadvertently: it happened to be wiretapping the Isa residence at the time because Zein Isa, Tina's father, was operating a cell of the Abu Nidal Organization (ANO), a Palestinian terrorist group from his home.[28] The wiretap caught the tragic murder and proved the parents' testimony as false: the parents told authorities that their daughter attacked them and that they killed her in self defence.

Such crimes are not outdated practices of former, archaic times like the 1980s. Honour killings and related crimes against women occur throughout the Muslim world. An estimated 4,000 women in Pakistan alone were murdered between 2001 and 2004. Perhaps a sign of progress, the government recently enacted a law banning honour killings, however, murders continue to occur and perpetrators have received lenient treatment even in cases where murder charges were brought. With sadness, the Human Rights Commission of Pakistan testifies that there is no evidence that honour killings have decreased since the law was instituted.[29] Lakhmira, a fifteen year old Pakistani girl, puts a name to the face of the suffering of many Islamic women. She fled for her life and was forced into hiding when she was attacked by family, declared a *kari*, literally meaning a *black-woman*, that is, a woman who has had sex outside of marriage. Her 40-year-old husband Dilawar, an influential member of the Shar tribe, declared her a *kari* after she wounded his pride when she admitted to others that his nephews were molesting her.[30] As an accused woman, Lakhmira's only options were vindication and mercy, or, if no one came to her rescue, a terrible fate she herself declared: "If someone does not come to our rescue I will commit suicide. In our culture it is impossible for a girl to live after being declared a *kari* even if it is a false charge. Only God knows the truth."[31]

INTERPRETATION MATTERS

Poor interpretations of the Quran not only oppress and objectify women, they also bind women to silly rules that are not necessary, argues Manji:

> Millions of Muslim women outside Arabia, including the West, veil themselves. They accept it as an act of spiritual submission. It's closer to cultural capitulation. Do you know where Iranian women got the design for their post-revolutionary chadors – the ones that don't let you reveal a wisp of your hair? From a Mullah who led the Shias in Lebanon. Now that's a heavy duty import. While the Quran requires the Prophet's wives to veil, it never decreed such a practice for all women. Why indeed should it? Veils protect women from sand and heat - not exactly a pressing concern beyond Arabia, Saharan Africa and the Australian outback. This means I could wear a turtleneck and a baseball cap to meet the theological demands of dressing modestly. To cover my face because that is what I am supposed to do, is nothing short of a brand of victory for desert Arabs, whose style has become the most trusted symbol of how to package yourself as a Muslim woman.[32]

Perhaps other passages in the Quran could be revisited and understood in new light that would mean greater freedom for Muslims. Yet, the Muslim holy book and its teachings are strictly adhered to by Muslim clerics and their followers. False reports, recently, that American soldiers used pages of the Quran as toilet paper in Guantanamo Bay,

Cuba resulted in mass protest and violence in Muslim dominated regions around the world. These events indicate that the Quran cannot be tampered with, interpreted, or touched by anyone other than those believers who uphold its unchanging, endorsed interpretation. The serious renovations within Islam that Manji foresees would free Muslims world-wide from fear, hunger, and illiteracy are not given the time of day by most Mullahs, scholars, and clerics.

Voices like Manji's, though, are easy for clerics and scholars to ignore. A woman, feminist, and lesbian, according to the Quran and in the same spirit of Tina Isa's parents, rather than listen to her, clerics should kill her: *Confront those women who are guilty of unbecoming conduct… confine them to their house until death overtakes them or Allah opens a way for them.*[33] Yet until voices such as Manji's are heard and Muslim leaders openly ask where verses in the Quran "come from, why they are contradictory, and how they can be differently interpreted" the question, why "no other religion is producing as many terrorists' travesties and human rights transgressions in the name of God?"[34] will remain a rhetorical one.

Winston Churchill considered Islam, a faith he observed was "far from moribund" but "militant and proselytizing," and foresaw its spread across the globe. The thought made him shudder:

> How dreadful are the curses which Mohammedanism lays on its votaries! Besides the fanatical frenzy, which is as dangerous in a man as hydrophobia in a dog, there is this fearful fatalistic apathy. The effects are apparent in many countries. Improvident habits, slovenly systems of agriculture, sluggish methods of commerce, and insecurity of property exist wherever the followers of the Prophet rule or live. A degraded sensualism deprives this

life of its grace and refinement; the next of its dignity and sanctity.[35]

What has prevented a religious system that spans fourteen centuries from transcending the barbaric tribalism that characterized it at its inception? Dr. Shorrosh suggests that Muhammad sentenced his followers to a state of perpetual barbarism because he did not call them to a higher way of life, but endorsed the traditional practices and customs of the desert: "murder, predatory war, slavery, polygamy, concubinage. Muhammad affirmed it to be the single portal whereby men could enter into Paradise. In a word, he took Arab people just as he found them, and declared all that they did to be very good and sacred from change."[36] Shorrosh observes that such as desert Arabs were when the prophet called them to the folds of Islam, so are Muslims now.

Perhaps Manji, Churchill, and Shorrosh make strange bedfellows, but their voices agree and ring with concern about the effects of militant and fanatic interpretations of the faith. The condition of the faith as it stands today, with all its crimes and cruelty against its own followers and humanity, reveals that "Islam is incapable of elevating a people to a higher level."[37]

CHAPTER SEVEN:
A CALL TO ACCOUNTABILITY

Let light shine out of the darkness

– Genesis 1: 3

ISLAM IN THE DEMOCRATIC WORLD

With Churchill, Manji, and many others, I too raise my voice. I believe it is time that Islam is held accountable in the public forum for its present day claims that it is a peaceful and holy religion. Where is the evidence? We must look at the Quran, yet we are told that as God's final and complete word to mankind it cannot be questioned. There seems so little room for truthful, intellectual discussion. What about the rights of women, what about justice and peace? We know that we cannot necessarily judge the theology of a religion by the behaviour of its participants;[1] a religion might teach one thing and yet its followers do another. If so, it is unfair to criticize the religion for the deviant behaviour of its so-called followers. Yet, what if followers practice what the religion and its very writings preach? We should have the right to connect behaviour with theology and therefore criticize the religion.

The recent murder of a Christian family in The United States perhaps suggests certain Muslims who say "peace" do not mean peace. On 13 January 2005, Hossam Armanious, his wife Amal, and two daughters, Sylvia and Monica, were found brutally murdered inside their Jersey City home. Armanious "would regularly debate religion in a Middle Eastern chat room" and was well known for "expressing his Coptic beliefs and engaging in fiery back-and-forth with Muslims on the Web site."[2] Armanious received threats that if he did not stop challenging Islamic beliefs on line, that he would be tracked down and "killed like a chicken."

The victims were tied up, their throats were slit, and Sylvia, one day short of her sixteenth birthday and known to be an outspoken Christian, was savagely mutilated. While Osama Hassan, director of the Islamic Center of Jersey City, describes the relationship between Copts and Muslims as cooperative if not friendly, though "there might be people that can get into physical fights," he does not think Muslims would be brought "to the point of murder."[3] Members of the Christian community, soon after the murders, lived in fear and did not believe for a moment the theory that the family fell victim to a robbery gone wrong: the perpetrators of the crime did not steal anything from the family's house. Instead, the slit throats of the slain seemed more like marks of Islamic jihad.[4] As the case goes to trial, that the killers were motivated to murder because of religious hate, is indicated by evidence such as the flesh gouged from Sylvia's wrist where she was tattooed with the Coptic cross.

Statements meant to assure us that Islam is peaceful, friendly, and safe should be questioned, especially in light of such stories of violence and discrimination performed in the name of Allah that are reported in the same press. Almost daily we receive reports from Iraq of suicide and car bombings, not against soldiers from the West, but by Iraqis against fellow Iraqi citizens. There may be room to debate that democracy is a Western value suddenly imposed upon people who may not have asked to raise its banner in their land, and yet we know the fall of Saddam Hussein's evil regime has meant new freedom for millions of Iraqis, a regime that unjustly starved, imprisoned, and killed countless citizens. Perhaps we do not have the right to desire democratic freedom, but it is right for us to desire that Iraqis live in peace. The recent election in the war-torn country was both encouraging and heartbreaking, and recent terrorism throughout the country against its own citizens reveals that the possibility of new freedom from fear and hopelessness will be difficult because of dangerous Muslim fanatics.

Why will success be difficult? Because in order to achieve democracy teachings of the Quran itself must be ignored or overturned, something Muslim fanatics will never allow. For instance, if the new Iraqi constitution is to give women the right to vote and represent the population at the governmental level a new trust and dignity of women is required, things the Quran and its interpreters find difficult: "Men are the protectors and maintainers of women because Allah has given more strength to men than women and because men support them from their means."[5] An example of how such doctrine is lived out in the West was reported recently in a recent documentary.

The film shows several different Muslims in the United States preparing to participate in their annual pilgrimage called the Hajj. One of those pilgrims was a new convert to Islam, a divorced woman who was Doctor of Physiology at a well known University. Before she could go on the pilgrimage she was required to have the permission of her husband or a man in her household. Without the permission of a man, the Islamic authorities would not authorize her Hajj. Because she was divorced and had no husband, the woman's hope of pilgrimage seemed dire, but a decision was made that the lone male in her household, her teen-age son, could grant her permission to attend the pilgrimage. An educated woman in the 'free' world is suddenly unable to make decisions about her spiritual well-being and personal freedom, but her young child can make such decisions for her because he is male.

Democracy seems like the only political solution able to reduce the threat of fanatical Islam, for it requires open debate, scrutiny, and compromise. Muslims live in democratic countries all over the world and use their democratic freedom, as they should, to practice their religion. What troubles me is that the extreme interpretation of Islam directly threatens democratic freedom. Muslim schools and mosques in Canada and the United States regularly promote fanaticism, hatred, and holy war against the West, and the courts keep clear of Islamic institutions that advocate Jihad. The media cries "racial discrimination" if Muslims are profiled and checked at security stations in airports, but few media outlets think it newsworthy to report that the same teachings and prayers that can be heard in the background of videos showing militant Muslims severing the heads of foreign hostages in Iraq are heard every day on North American soil from Islamic prayer towers.

Kofi Annan's recent request of the United Nations General Assembly to recognize Hezbollah as a legal governing entity both legitimizes and intensifies my concern. Hezbollah, with a well trained, equipped fighting force of 25,000 soldiers and both spiritual and financial support from millions of Muslims world-wide, is one of the most violent Islamic terrorist organizations in the world today. That the Secretary General of the United Nations would make such a request gives credit to the criticism of some authorities that the United Nations in the hands of Arab and third world or ex-communist countries. One such critic notes:

> The U.N. has condemned Israel more than any other country in the world, including the regime of Castro, Idi Amin or Kaddahfi. By behaving this way, the U.N. leaves a door open by not openly condemning terrorist organizations. In addition, through UNRWA [United Nations Relief and Works Agency], the U.N. is directly tied to terror organizations such as Hamas, representing 65 percent of their apparatus in the so-called Palestinian refugee camps. As a support to Arab countries, the U.N. has maintained Palestinians in camps with the hope to "return" into Israel for more than 50 years, therefore making it impossible to settle those populations, which still live in deplorable conditions. Four hundred million dollars are spent every year, mainly financed by U.S. taxes, to support 23,000 employees of UNRWA, many of whom belong to terrorist organizations.[6]

The political agenda of Hezbollah is the complete annihilation of Israel. The United States is also on their list of destruction; soldiers can be heard chanting, "Death to America, Death to Israel!" in the streets. Essentially, Annan's request that Hezbollah be recognized as a legitimate governing entity in Palestine undermines the mandate of the United Nations, any peace keeping efforts in the Middle East, and the principles of democracy. The thought of a United Nations-endorsed Hezbollah is ironic. The United Nations denounced the war in Iraq, yet might be willing to recognize a governing body whose genetic makeup as an organization puts Muslims on a war path.

Neville Chamberlain, then Prime Minister of Great Britain, said "Peace for our time" as he proudly held a document signed by Adolf Hitler as he stepped from a plane on 30 September, 1938. How will the West fare when, God forbid, it must fight a significant Muslim force that the democratic West has itself endorsed, equipped, and fuelled, both politically and ideologically? Word War II, in today's currency, cost the United States twelve trillion dollars and saw 500,000 men killed in action. These staggering figures perhaps would have been reduced had the warning signs of the Nazi threat been taken more seriously in the pre-war years. The United Sates has spent one hundred twenty billion dollars on the war in Iraq and lost 2000 men, two-thirds of the 3000 innocent lives lost in the 9/11 attacks, symbolic attacks made against the United States, the poster child of democracy, for its support of Israel.[7] The war against terrorism is on, yet so few in the West are willing to fight it. What future debt will we accumulate, in numbers of dollars and lives, for an enemy who will not disappear through wishful thinking or pleasing political rhetoric?

SUBMISSION

History seems to repeat itself; how frightening that the biggest threat to peace, human dignity, democracy, and a life without fear since Nazi Germany also has a specific agenda to see the end of the Jewish race. Who are the great men and women, like Winston Churchill, who perceived the growing threat of fascism in the 1930s and then the threat of Communism in his "Iron Curtain" speech in 1946, that will be remembered in history as heroes, though they were once ignored, even maligned?

For me, one of the most frightening accounts of what fanatical Islam enacts as it encounters democratic freedom took place on 2 November 2004 in Holland when a Moroccan born Muslim and Dutch citizen gruesomely murdered filmmaker Theo van Gogh. Mohammed Bouyeri, the killer, fired six gunshots into van Gogh as he bicycled along an Amsterdam bike path. Wounded and bleeding, van Gogh pleaded for mercy and attempted to engage his assailant in conversation. Bouyeri diplomatically responded by cutting van Gogh's throat, nearly severing his head from his body. Then, to complete his evil act, the murderer pinned a five page letter of protest on Van Gogh's chest with a Bowie knife. The letter promised that "hair-raising screams will be squeezed from the lungs of non-believers" and contained names of prominent Dutch citizens, including a Jewish mayor and several Members of Parliament, scheduled for murder. What was the reason for van Gogh's violent death? A ten minute film entitled "Submission" that the director made with a Liberal Member of Parliament, Somali refugee and former Muslim Ayaan Hirshi Ali. "Submission" tells the story of a Muslim woman forced into an arranged marriage, abused by her husband, and raped by an uncle. A scene in the film shows the woman's naked body through her clothing covered with welts from a whipping as well as passages from the Quran written on her skin.[8]

The Dutch have not faced such evil since the occupying Germans invaded the Netherlands during World War II. In fear of further violence, the movie was banned from theatres. Suddenly the freedom of artistic expression was suspended in the country. Horrified by the act of violence and afraid of future incidents the barbaric act by a Muslim was denounced by a Muslim cleric, who concluded that the act was somehow expected because of the film's obvious offence to Islam.[9]

Suddenly the ever "politically correct" Dutch population are faced with a very real and frightening Islamic threat. The 15 million Dutch now regard the one million resident Muslims with genuine fear. And why shouldn't they? A recent poll indicates that 300,000 of the resident Muslims in Holland fervently support radical Muslim centres and schools.[10] Muslim clerics publicly denounce violence and yet in the same sentence explain it away, even condone it. Islam means "complete submission." The story of van Gogh is one example of those consequences unfavourable explorations of Islam that doubters and critics with receive at the hand of Muslims loyal to the Quran. Van Gogh's story shows us one possibility of what complete submission to Allah really looks like in our world.

Chapter Eight: A Call to Action

It is very easy to hate a Nazi, guardian in a Gulag.
But the real danger is not them. It is decent people
who compromise with evil.

— Jacobo Timerman

ENABLERS OF EVIL

When Ayat Akras, a Palestinian girl, walked into a crowded supermarket in Jerusalem and detonated the explosives strapped to her body, she maimed twenty-five innocent bystanders, and killed herself and two others. She also became a hero in the Muslim world. Her extreme act of devotion to Allah inspired a poem written by the Saudi Arabian ambassador to the United Kingdom:

> Tell Ayat the bride of loftiness...
> She embraced death with a smile...
> While the leaders are running away from death,
> Doors of heaven are open for her.
>
> You (Ayat) died to honor God's word.
> You committed suicide?
> We committed suicide by living,
> Like the dead.[1]

The world is threatened by the concerted effort of radical Muslims to see it bow in submission to Allah. Ultimately, jihad is the central duty of every Muslim. The word has different interpretations and meanings to modern Muslim theologians, one of which is "the defense of the faith from critics."[2] And yet, rather than being quick to denounce murder, rape, torture, and terror, major Muslim groups deny unbelievers as well as Muslim women equality, human rights, and dignity. Violent jihad cannot accept criticism and cannot defend its position with honest reflection and debate. It cannot exist in a true democracy within the boundaries of its mandate.

Emerick assures that Islam condemns the following sins:

- ◆ Committing idolatry
- ◆ Stealing from an orphan
- ◆ Committing adultery and fornication
- ◆ Accusing a chaste woman falsely
- ◆ Giving false testimony
- ◆ Committing murder and suicide
- ◆ Enslaving a free person [3]

Although these sins are denounced in word by Islam, they are not altogether denounced in deed, and have been committed in the name of Allah since Muhammad lifted his sword in the desert. Furthermore, these sins are sanctioned by the Quran and related Islamic sacred writings.

In places like Sudan under Omar Hassan al Turabi, leader of the Muslim Brotherhood, an organization that condemns the above sins in word, unbelievers have been raped, tortured, orphaned, kidnapped, and killed. How many more husbands and fathers will witness the rape of their wives, sisters, and daughters, their last earthly sight before they submit to the sword of jihad? How many more children will have their parents stolen from them and enslaved? How many more women will be falsely accused of adultery or fornication and then be left to the mercy of the powers that be? In Iran and other Muslim countries, how many more Mullahs will accept money to arrange marriages that last merely as long as the bridegroom desires: a day, one month, a lifetime? How many more young men will take their own lives and the lives of others in hopes of escaping the drudgery and plight of this world for the pleasures of eternal sexual bliss? How will the world see an end to violent, tragic suicides if young Muslim school children throughout the world believe without doubt that such "martyrs" directly enter paradise?

Mahmoud Ahmadinejad, Iran's president, recently denounced attempts to recognize Israel or normalize relations with it. Referring to the October 2005 suicide bombing which claimed five Israeli lives and injured many others, at a conference in Tehran called "The World without Zionism," Ahmadinejad said,

> There is no doubt that the new wave (of attacks) in Palestine will wipe off this stigma (Israel) from the face of the Islamic world.... Anybody who recognizes Israel will burn in the fire of the Islamic nation's fury, any (Islamic leader) who recognizes the Zionist regime means he is acknowledging the surrender and defeat of the Islamic world.[4]

Quoting an Imam at the conference, the Iranian president concluded that Israel must be "wiped off the map."

These are the sins of Islam; this is what the prophet Muhammad's religion offers the world. Political and spiritual leaders in the Islamic world endorse and call for the end of entire people groups, and show no qualms about it, defying anyone who stands in their way. Such radical Muslim zeal pits all unlike thinkers against itself. Simply recognizing the basic right of a people to name itself a nation makes one an enemy of leaders like Ahmadinejad. We have gone out for a night at the theatre, closed our eyes as the lights dimmed, and found ourselves in the middle of a war. Whether we choose to fight or not, we have been thrown into the middle of it. Bombs in London, bombs in Israel, bombs in Baghdad, bombs in New York. No amount of blinking, or wishing, or pinching our own skin will make it disappear. So, what will we do?

English philosopher Edmund Burke said that the only thing necessary for the triumph of evil was for good men to do nothing. I believe what we are witnessing today is evil in one of its finest hours: Satan at war in the heavens, the backdrop of humanity's existence. Evil is at work, so who are its "enablers?"

We are: Christians, Jews, Muslims alike, and all others who do not identify with these faiths. We live in a politically correct, multicultural world where a very interesting phenomenon occurs: some statements even if they are true, simply cannot be said, or, if said, will not be taken seriously. Plainly, every good person in our world today who excuses Muslim acts of terrorism as the result of a few misguided, disenfranchised men who subvert Islam, contribute to the problem. Brigitte Gabriel reminds us that:

> We are faced with a war that has been declared on Christians and Jews in America and the world. Citizens of the most powerful country on earth watched in horror on 9/11, 2001 as a handful of men brought the United States of America to its knees. Wall Street froze, the stock market tumbled, and international air traffic ground to a halt. The West faces a threat more menacing today than the past goals of communist domination.

> We are facing an enemy that uses children as human bombs, mothers as suicide bombers, and men driven by the glory of death and the promise of eternal sexual bliss in heaven. We are fighting an enemy that loves death more than we love life.[5]

In Sweden a Christian pastor was recently given a jail sentence for preaching that according to scripture, homosexuality is a sin. The wonders of modern secular society have decided that such a statement means the Bible includes hate literature. But the scholarship stops there and pays no attention to the Bible's stance that all sin can be forgiven by God and all Christians are to love sinners. And yet the Quran has pages rife with words of outright hatred. The Quran describes how in most cases people ought to be killed for their sin, not forgiven. Where is the public debate on this matter?

The following statement is rarely, if ever said publicly: *We are at war with Islam!* Even though, at its heart, in the Quran Islam considers all non-Muslims Infidels who must be brought under submission to Allah or be killed, we dare not say we are at war with Islam. We do not believe it though the religion's writings teach the fact over and over again. We are at war, even if we do not want to be, because Islam has declared war on us.

When Islamic terror strikes, we report and count the dead. We look at devastating pictures recorded by our media and news reporters. We listen to many so-called experts as they explain their points of view. We watch our world attacked bit by small bit and conclude: "a small minority of misguided zealots." The number might be small in comparison to the millions of Muslims who truly desire peace, but we fail to connect the zealous acts with the teachings at the heart of Islam. The war takes place politically between Islam and the Western world, but it also takes place between Muslims as well. Anyone who resists or disagrees with the doctrine of death is "other" and, ultimately, an enemy of Islam.

The recent suicide bombing by an Iraqi citizen in Jordan illustrates the point. Jordan is a Muslim country but has taken a side against militant Islam. Though Muslim, Jordan has not been spared from the threat of retribution. All that a Muslim nation or person needs to do is show compassion or diplomacy towards Israel or the United States and as a result that society or person is considered a traitor to Islam.

Ironically, George Bush has failed to identify Islam as the real source of the terrorism we face. Whether because of ignorance or political expediency, he continues to refer to Islam as a peaceful religion. He has often referred to the innocence of the Muslim religion and blamed the continued acts of terrorism as a result of those that have taken the religion hostage.

Political parties, governments, and the media are unwilling or are incapable of calling today's terrorism a war declared by Islam. The culture, as a whole, seems incapable of identifying spiritual evil. Nazism started as an expression of occult activity. The German people as well as most of Europe were unable to identify the spiritual root of the evil cult. As a result a small group eventually saw an entire nation ruled by evil. In the same way, evil is at work in our world today, and yet few are willing or capable of saying so. I fear that lack of discernment will bring entire societies and nations to their knees in submission to the militant demands of Islam.

Brigitte Gabriel explains that during the war years in Lebanon, Christian churches were often destroyed and desecrated. She describes incidents where Christian pastors were murdered by Muslims, who then proceeded to defecate on the church altar and use the pages of the Bible for toilet paper. These were not isolated incidents. Christian and Jewish Holy sites are in constant danger and threat of desecration by militant Muslims. Each day Muslims slaughter innocent humans in service of Allah. On 19 October 2005 three Christian girls were slaughtered on their way to a Christian school in Indonesia by Muslims. They were all beheaded in Islamic fashion and one of the severed heads was left in front of the local Christian church.

The news article that reported this Satanic evil asked Christians to pray for the families and the evil doers. Their response was compassionate and Christian. I believe, however, that there is room for Christians and society in general to take a more severe approach. Force of some degree is required to protect innocents from such evil acts. If a child was attacked by a sexual predator, any one, including a professing Christian, would receive a hero's welcome for physically intervening and seeing a child set free from the evil grasp of a paedophile.

THREE MUSKETEERS

When World War II was over and I was a young adult I learned that not everyone in my childhood neighbourhood was on the winning side of the war. In every war there are traitors; in Holland there were many. The ideas Hitler proclaimed were, by many Dutch, seen as a necessity for change. As a nation we were closer in ideology to Germans then we were to the British. We were, first of all, neighbours that shared a common border, and spoke a similar language. For centuries the Dutch had been at war for colonies against the British.

I grew up reading the great stories of how our countrymen withstood the struggle for South Africa during the Boer War. As a very young boy I learned to love the stories of how the Boers defeated the British in battles even when they were outnumbered. The Boers were my heroes, the English my childhood enemy.

For me, World War II changed all of that very quickly. My father who was in the police force during the German attack did not have time to report to his army regiment. The German attack was so sudden and unexpected that any fighting between the Germans and Dutch occurred over a period of five disoriented days. My father spoke of the thousands of German paratroopers that filled the sky and often mentioned witnessing a German paratrooper kill an innocent person riding his bike as he watched the parachutes land.

As one of the policemen captured by the Nazi's, my father was instructed to continue to maintain basic law and order in the city of Delft. At some point, my father was contacted by the Underground to help in the cause, secretly defying the Germans. But not all policemen on the force showed the same national honour. In many ways it was in the best interests of a policeman's family to submit and work alongside the Germans showing no resistance. There was no outstanding reason to believe that Germany would fail in its war effort. If, as predicted, the Germans won the war it would be in the best interest of the family to be found a loyal servant to Germany. The similarities in language and geography, perhaps, made such decisions that much easier.

In a war you must choose sides. If you were for Hitler, at some point you had to be willing to turn your Jewish neighbours in to the Nazis. At some point, my father and mother made a choice. The consequence of their choice meant, if their true loyalties were discovered, they would be executed by the Nazis.

But choosing to take the side for the Nazi's eventually also had its risk. To be found out as a collaborator could mean your execution. I recall the story of three brothers in my home town of Delft. They became known as the "Three Musketeers." The three brothers, along with Underground co-workers pretended to be German sympathizers. If certain persons in our town were suspected as traitors of Holland, they would approach them, act as German spies, and commend them for their work. If it became obvious that those they suspected were indeed German collaborators, they would execute them and bury the traitors in their own back yards. I often wonder what the three brothers were like before an evil time required them to act in the way they did. I also wonder if, in our day, we will once again see such horrible times.

When my dad was in hiding, my mother, younger sister, and I were often moved to different locations to hide. Late in the war we were in our own home again and my mother was secretly listening to the BBC on the radio, an act strictly forbidden by the Germans. A neighbour, sympathetic to the Nazi's, spoke to my mother and warned her to stop, an interaction that created a great amount of fear in the house: would our neighbour tell the Germans?

Once again my favourite uncle, Dad's younger brother who provided us with food when there was little food to find, came to the rescue.

Dressed in a trench coat and pretending that he held concealed weapons, he confronted the neighbour and threatened to execute and bury him in his backyard. Such a fate was, by then, a real possibility because the "Three Musketeers" were known and feared in our town. The bluff, a risk my uncle made in the desperate situation, worked. Our neighbour begged for his life. My uncle granted the neighbour's request on the condition that if there was ever a threat against his sister-in-law again, it would mean certain death.

I have often recollected the story. What frightening and desperate circumstances. But the times, though undesirable, called for such measures. In that horrible war there came a point where people had to choose sides and act in ways they would never imagine in more peaceful times. When we wake up to the reality of war, which side will we choose? As innocent people are once again slaughtered, what drastic measures will we take? May we have the discernment to recognize perilous times and the courage to live bravely in them.

I believe Christians and non-Christians alike need discernment when we should go beyond a "pray for the enemy" approach. The heinous actions that are carried out against innocent humans by depraved Muslims deserve a serious response. Otherwise, by not responding to the wide-spread Islamic evil that is escalating daily we will revisit horrors of the past. How many more people must die before we are mobilized again behind the mantra *Never Again?*

"There is therefore, about all complete conviction a kind of huge helplessness. The belief is so big that it takes a long time to get into action. And this hesitation chiefly arises, oddly enough, from an indifference about where one should begin."[6] What will finally convince us to change? What action will we take against the evils in this world?

CHAPTER NINE:
A CALL TO DISCERNMENT AND ALERTNESS

With his lips an enemy speaks sweetly, but in his heart he schemes to plunge you into the abyss. Though your enemy has tears in his eyes, if given the chance, he will never have enough of your blood.

— Sirach 12: 10-18

Pearl Harbor and Beyond

I once was completely confident that I would be ready to defend my loved ones, as necessary, in times of greatest need and crisis. A few times, however, that self-confidence has been shattered. I recall, in particular, a time when living on my small farm with my wife and children I was unprepared to defend my family in the way I thought I could.

Our small stock farm was close to a local ski hill where a weekend rock concert was organized. When the event came to the ski hill, it became apparent that police were not prepared for the various resulting security issues. Our neighbours' farms which were located closer to the event than my own farm were overrun by people, most of whom were in altered states of consciousness because of drug and alcohol abuse. I spent most of the day marching around my neighbours' farms watching in disgust and frustration as unruly people wreaked havoc and destruction: fences were torn down, property was damaged, and the perpetrators left garbage, broken glass, and debris everywhere. Thousands of people, in a blitz of uncontrolled humanity, left their mark on the farmland. As the day came to a close, I went home to my nearby farm, in a state of vigilant preparedness. I anticipated the very real possibility that my home would become an overnight target for similar vandalism, even theft as the concert readied for its second night. I sent my family to the nearby town where they would be safe and decided to sleep with one eye open, and protect my farm if I must.

Although I felt prepared to wake at the slightest suggestion of mischief as I went to bed that night, I slept like a dead man! The next day I got a phone call from a friend who apologised to me for intruding on my property. His son was at the rock concert, and, after a late night of music, needed a ride home. Needing to use a phone, he came to my house, knocked on your door, came in, hollered, but found no one at home. So, he used my phone to call his father, my apologetic friend, who came to pick him up. My friend learned that I was, in fact, home. He felt bad that he too had hollered up the stairs where I slept so late at night to see if I was home.

I have never forgotten this embarrassing event. It made me realize how vulnerable I was left to my own devices. That night the very thing I thought that I was most prepared for – intrusion on my own property – was, in reality, the very thing I was least prepared for.

Our North American and Western society is exactly in this state of self presumed alertness; in reality people are fast asleep. There is little acknowledgement of the very real danger that has made its appearance in our lives, and shown up on our own soil. Some compare the 9/11 attacks to the attacks by the Japanese in World War II at Pearl Harbour. The unfortunate response at that time saw Americans respond in fear, suspicious that all Japanese in their neighbourhoods were the possible enemy. The seizure of property and the imprisonment of entire Japanese families became an embarrassing human tragedy whose wounds have taken years to heal.

In retrospect, the internment of Japanese-American citizens was improper, yet given the times the response cannot totally be condemned as a human failure. It was a knee-jerk response to a sudden and unexpected threat. We must learn from history, and we have learned from the North American response to Pearl Harbour. Is it possible, though, to over-learn a lesson? At present, the pendulum seems to swing in the exact opposite direction to an equally or more dangerous position. The media is rife with the idea that the observation of mosques by governments and careful inspection of Muslims at security points is an unfair display of racial profiling of post-Pearl Harbour proportions.

We must be discerning, sensitive, and alert. Osama Bin Laden has reportedly named a goal to see at least four million Americans, two million of whom must be children, killed on American soil. "Only then," bin Laden has said, "would the crimes committed by America on the Arab and Muslim world be avenged."[1] The claim by Paul L. Williams, a former FBI consultant, that former CIA Director George Tenet informed President Bush after the 9/11 attacks that two "suitcase" nuclear bombs have reached al-Qaida operatives in the United States with enough fissionable plutonium and uranium to produce an explosion yield in excess of two kilotons is alarming. Williams claims that there is virtually no doubt among intelligence analysts that al-Qaida has acquired fully assembled nuclear weapons. The only question is how many have already been smuggled into the United States?[2]

The possibility of such a real and deadly threat is terrifying, to say the least. If there is any validity to such claims, is not a degree of profiling and surveillance of Muslims acceptable for the sake of the freedom and security of entire nations?

Ironically, the very people whose religion has declared war on America and the free world often use unfortunate travel delays as well as personal information searches as offenses against their human rights. The case of Mahar Arar a Canadian Muslim, is an example. Arar was arrested on one of his out-of-the-country trips, questioned, and sent to Syria by the United States government with the approval of the Canadian government. At the time, soon after the 9/11 terrorist attacks, Mr. Arar was a terrorist suspect. During his time in Syria, he was tortured. At present, he has been cleared of terrorist charges.

If Arar was treated unfairly, that is by and of itself unfortunate. Canadian Muslims, Mr. Arar and his wife who holds a doctoral degree in economics, are exhibited regularly on CBC television. Canada watches with interest, and perhaps some shock, that the couple is suing the Canadian government for 400 million dollars.

The case, before the courts, seems an ironic turning of the tables.

Allegedly Canada, wakened to the horror of Islamic terrorism in North America and with certain information provided by its southern neighbour, responded in dangerous times to a threat and released a citizen into American and Syrian custody. The recent statement by a retired CSIS agent that Canada has over 50 active Islamic terrorist groups within its own borders confirms that certain Muslims in Canada are real threats to North American citizens. The suffering Arar experienced, a solitary incident, is terrible, but given the times, the cooperation of the Canadian government to its American allies is understandable. A 400 million dollar lawsuit is not, and suggests an insensitivity to the times.

Arar and others might cry foul at the temporary suspension of their freedom, while, in the meantime, Muslim leaders, clerics, and believers openly call for an increased jihad: an increase of Muslim soldiers willing to die as suicide bombers because America has violated the sacred soil of Islam by attacking Iraq.

A CALL TO DISCERNMENT

Muslims are quick to take full advantage of the freedom of religion which is practiced throughout the Western world. For example, France had one mosque in 1974. Now there are more than 1500 mosques in France. The generous freedoms offered to Muslims in the Western world, however, are completely reversed in countries where Islamic governments rule. In Islamic countries, Christian missionaries are forbidden to preach to Muslims. Some governments prohibit any kind of Christian activity whatsoever. In Saudi Arabia you must be a Muslim to obtain citizenship.[3] We in the West have "fouled our own nest" by giving time or place to the insistent belief that we are to blame for the ill-felt feelings that Muslims harbour against the West.

Islam has declared war on the non-Islamic world for quite some time. 9/11 should have been our greatest wake up call ever. The murderers flying the planes lived in our neighbourhoods. For years on end they lived unnoticed, well-mannered, as full participants in Western life; nothing in their daily behaviour gave away their evil intentions to unsuspecting neighbours. Yet every secret moment of their lives, they determined to destroy the Western way of life. We were played the fool.

After Pearl Harbour we locked up and interned Japanese citizens. Those imprisoned were innocent. After 9/11 we have allowed ourselves to be taken captive by an altruistic but inane tolerance. We must learn from history, that is, we must use discernment and caution. We must learn from history: we must be wary of very real threats. Every Muslim who desires to participate as a free citizen in the Western world, because of the times, should invite the utmost scrutiny of their religious and personal lives necessary to ensure security and freedom, in accordance with the law.

Certain critics of Islam voice their concern less subtly:

> While it is absolutely appropriate for Westerners to practice tolerance of immigrants, Islamic migrants, not all but many, bring with them a duty to participate in Muhammad's fantasy of an Islamic planet earth. There is no sense in wasting time trying to "change the mind-set" of this culture. They are a driven people. Driven by backward, racist, sexist ideology, directed by the Quran – with terror networks, Muslim advocacy organizations, imams, and clerics serving as reminders to Muslims.
>
> Islamophobia, paranoia, and intolerance have nothing to do with it. The facts speak plainly for themselves....

Not all Muslims appear to be so hell bent on this, but since they sit silently on the sidelines, deciphering the difference between them shouldn't be our responsibility....While it's nice to be nice, why should anyone want to demonstrate kindness to those who would just as soon cut our throats to obtain what the Quran commands them to obtain?

While tolerance is a good thing, tolerance of the intolerant is suicidal. There must come a time when we must recognize a threat which, if not eliminated, could end our existence as we know it. That time would be right about now.[4]

Perhaps any attempt by a Muslim to complain about racial profiling and abuse should be seen as a red flag and monitored by the appropriate officials. We do not want to live in a state of paranoia, but we must be wise. The enemy of the new war cannot be identified as one group of people that share a culture and country: enemies with a border. The new enemy has spread throughout every culture and country in the world. In the societies where they originated they have left tyranny and every human failure. Somehow we are expected to believe that the societies and cultures Islam has migrated to will accomplish different feats. I am afraid that we in North America and the West have become Secular Enablers. In an effort to prove that we will never repeat the unfortunate error that was our response to fellow citizens after Pearl Harbour, we risk a greater tragedy: the end of the very freedom we have known in the West. We feel humane and evolved for inviting Islam to announce its faith from minarets. We feel good and tolerant for declaring that Islam is a peaceful religion. Do we shudder at the real possibility of nuclear and suicide bombs, not in a foreign country, but in our own backyard? Is it inappropriate to ask, even demand, that Islam, if it is to take advantage of Western freedom, rise to a new level of transparency and accountability?

CHAPTER TEN: ROADBLOCKS TO PROGRESS

Treason (noun): Violation of the allegiance owed to one's sovereign state; betrayal of ones country.

In his book *Heretics*, G.K. Chesterton underscored what little progress the contemporary thinkers of the early 1900s had made when they abandoned orthodoxy and proudly put on the robes of heresy.

> When everything about a people is for the time growing weak and ineffective, it begins to talk about efficiency. So it is that when a man's body is a wreck he begins, for the first time, to talk about health.
>
> Vigorous organisms talk not about their processes, but about their aims. There cannot be any better proof of the physical efficiency of a man than that he talks cheerfully of a journey to the end of the world. And there cannot be any better proof of the practical efficiency of a nation than that it talks constantly of a journey to the end of the world, a journey to the Judgment Day and the New Jerusalem.… The time of big theories was the time of big results. In the era of sentiment and fine words, at the end of the eighteenth century, men were really robust and effective.[1]

Chesterton observed much of humanity lost faith in his day and in doing so lost the world. He connects the language we use to describe ourselves and our vision for the future as a signal about our state of health as individuals and nations. I suspect Chesterton would not give us a clean bill of health but might ask, instead, *Where are the big ideas, the fine words, the wonderful sentiment – that vision of the New Jerusalem at the end of the world?* We have lost these things and replaced them with an efficient vocabulary of political correctness.

When people hesitate to plainly speak their opinions for fear they might be unpopular or intolerant, truth is threatened, it is shackled and hamstrung. When politicians, especially at campaign time, focus more on what *not* to say rather than what they think and value, aware that a careless deviation outside of the politically correct landscape will create an inevitable media outrage, there is a problem. People seem weak, intimidated by the possibility of unpopularity, rather than "robust and effective."

World leaders take their shoes off at the holy ground of tolerance and politically correct speech, and tip toe carefully in awe of its mysterious power. The realities of globalism and the multi-cultural, mutli-religious communities it produces compound the difficulty of leading and living in a way that respects individuals. While religious freedom, multiculturalism, and political correctness can be good principles to practice, they are dangerous when applied liberally and dogmatically in all situations. They can be like strong hands that grip the throats or cover the mouths of people who observe things that cause concern and would like to raise their voice. To state, factually, that 17 Muslim men in Toronto planned to kill the Prime Minister is interpreted by some as ethnic and religious discrimination and the same offended ears are quick to argue that "not all Muslims are terrorists" though the assumption was never made. Facts are made hot-button issues and in the name of political correctness, for some reason, accurate statements can make everyone walk on egg-shells.

In a secular, post-Christian society it should come as no surprise that secularists do not recognize or identify evil and that secularists cannot accept that there might be a root of spiritual evil in Islamic theology. Christians, however, should be shocked at the same ignorance of the secularists exists within the Church. *Little children, do not be ignorant of the wiles of the devil*[2]*; but be wise as serpents and harmless or innocent as doves.*[3] For the most part Christians have figured out how to be harmless, but many lack wisdom.

Brigitte Gabriel highlights that historically important organizations and denominations, such as the Presbyterian Church USA (PCUSA), show in their ventures into international politics that they have lost moral discernment:

> In the last few years the PCUSA leadership befriended Husballah, one of the world's most lethal terrorist organizations solely responsible for killing Americans in Beirut in 1983 when a truck bomb blew up the Marine barracks killing over 241 soldiers and civilians. This was the greatest slaughter of Americans prior to Al-Qaeda demolishing the World Trade Center September 11, 2001. Husballah's weekly chants, prayers and speeches of "Death to America, Death to America", are broadcast 24/7 from Lebanon and the world through their satellite TV station, Al-Manar.
>
> Gabriel also examines the PCUSA's decision to call its members to divest from companies doing business with Israel because it considers the security barrier between Jew and Palestinian to be another sign of Israeli occupation making worse the plight of Palestinians. Gabriel states that beyond standing up for Palestine "by considering divestment, the PCUSA has also become the defender and champion of Palestinian suicide bombers headed by the terror group Hamas an affiliate of the Muslim Brotherhood" which experts estimate has sleeper terrorist cells in over forty American states.

Gabriel asks "[has] the PCUSA leadership lost their collective conscience and sense of right versus wrong?" The security barrier is a defensive response by a sovereign nation to Palestinians who:

penetrate Israel without [conscience or] humanity in order to maim and kill random Israelis. Since its creation,
the security barrier has prevented thousands of attacks
saving untold innocent civilians. Penalizing Israel for protecting the lives of its men, women and children is like
penalizing a woman who has been raped repeatedly along
with her children for putting up a security system in her
home to stop the rapists. The PCUSA is acting as if the
rights of criminals committing these suicidal acts over-
ride the rights of the innocents to protect themselves.

While the PCUSA's dislike of the security barrier might be admirable,
it's condemnation of Israel is troubling and though sensible in politically
correct times, is short-sighted. Gabriel reminds us that Israel is not to
the cause of Palestinian suffering, no matter what organizations like
Hezbollah or Hamas might announce.

The sad reality is that Palestinians are suffering because
of their corrupt leadership. Since 1993 and the sign-
ing of the Oslo Accord, billions of dollars have poured
into the Palestinian Authority to help them build in-
frastructure, improve the economy, build schools, etc.
The money went to line the pockets of their corrupt
leaders while the Palestinians were living like rats. For
years they have been left in squalor to be the ugly poster
child of Israeli aggression. All that the world sees is poor
people bemoaning their wretched lives. They don't see
that the Palestinian's plight has been brought on by its all
consuming hatred driven by Islamic radicalism, racism,
bigotry, and intolerance to see the Jews destroyed.

Gabriel concludes that the PCUSA's "support for intolerant victimizers who prey on the suffering they cause their own people make them accomplices to this evil."[4]

The excerpts from above article are a serious indictment of a mainline church for its social and political associations. The Presbyterian Church in Tthe United States is an accomplice to evil not because it has compassion for Palestinians, a sentiment which is good and right. It is an accomplice to evil because it lends support to evil terrorist and political groups that exist to see the death of another nation. In a sense, the PCUSA is being treasonous. In former times, the act of treason was easily distinguished and appropriately punished. In our day, this is no longer true. Things once considered treasonous are cloaked or veiled under false pretences like the freedom of speech and information. Supporting terrorist groups who mean to destroy society violates the allegiance expected of any democratic citizen.

APOSTASY, HERESY, AND UNDERSTANDING THE TIMES

Most people have the ability to discern between things that are erroneous and things that are true. For Christians this should be a spiritual inheritance. Much of my research into Islam required that I browse the internet. For me, research in this web of information was a very new and somewhat cumbersome experience, not without a few surprises or bizarre coincidences. One site I found on Islam had a 'pop-up' advertisement. The purpose of pop-ups are to entice people to buy into similar thoughts, interests, or products. And there on my screen was a pop-up with information about a special speaker called Reverend Sponge. The article spoke of the church where he would speak, his topic was on a "Revised Understanding of Christianity."

As I began to read more about Reverend Sponge's theological position,

I began to realize the man was a wolf in sheep's clothing, a heretic through and through, posing in a clerical collar. Now it might seem no small thing to call someone a heretic, and that such name calling would encourage an emotional response by the heretic himself. But what I discovered was that the name-calling brought no offence. I contacted the church where Reverend Sponge was scheduled to speak and made it very clear that, based on his online information, I expected Mr. Sponge was going to present fabricated lies about Christian doctrine to a vulnerable and unsuspecting audience: people seeking the truth about Christianity.

Sponge and his followers are a group of apostate ministers and main-line church leaders that meet annually in California. They deny the Virgin birth of Jesus, as well as His death and resurrection. They then proceed to meet and go through the Gospels and they vote on which Gospel they believe is true, may be true, or which Gospel is false. Then they rewrite their understanding of the Scriptures and teach their heretical theology to new and misguided minds.

In the no nonsense e-mail that I sent to the church located in one of the eastern United States, I received a very accommodating, even politically correct reply. I was thanked for my letter and questions and was told that the particular church was interested in bringing out different points of view on understanding the Scriptures. The church was so tolerant of my intolerance! And that is how we are losing the most important battles of our day. We, especially Christians, are losing the battle for truth.

My awareness of the fact that truth is slipping through our hands was confirmed to me during a conversation I had with my friendly pharmacist. My pharmacist is a part time minister in the United Church. He still preaches at times. I often spoke in friendly conversations with the man, and in the course of one such conversation learned the sad news that he had recently lost his wife to cancer and that he was now spending most of his time studying of Christian theology. As we talked I mentioned my recent studies and research into the Islamic religion and suggested there was evil lurking in Islam at its roots. My statement was immediately rebutted with, "Oh no! Islam is a most peaceful religion!"

I was shocked. Immediately I began to ask some theological questions. His answers came like a flood. The Gospels, he said, were a made up account: Jesus and His disciples realized that they were in danger and began to create a false history that was recorded in the Gospels for whatever reason. I suddenly blurted out, "That sounds like the heresy Reverend Sponge seems to be teaching out of California!" To which he responded, "Oh, you've heard of the Reverend? He's a fine man and wonderful theologian." My pharmacist, the part-time theologian and minister, as it were, belongs to the heretical group out of California.

I admit that at this point I became so disturbed and angry I could have spit nails! My pharmacist continues to treat me so nicely. He mentions special speakers I might be interested to hear. He knows that I think his theology is despicably heretical, and that I think his group uses their clerical collars to teach "weak vessels" gross spiritual lies.

What shocks and concerns me most of all is the misinformation that some important thinkers who have sound Christian doctrine provide. *Messiah and the Three Faiths of Jerusalem*, a recent documentary by RBC Ministries which publishes the popular devotional *Our Daily Bread*, identified that Judaism, Christianity, and Islam share a common root: the three faiths await the arrival of the Messiah. Islam, the program declared, awaits the return of Jesus as do Christians. Much effort is made in the documentary to prove the similarities and common ground Jews, Christians, and Muslims share, and likely the purpose of these comparisons is to build bridges toward dialogue and understanding, rather than to burn them which, historically, has often been the status quo of inter-faith dialogue.

The RBC's effort to underline similarities, however, is dangerous, as important facts are not mentioned in the effort to uncover common ground. Islam does, for instance, await the coming of Jesus, but it does not consider him to be the Messiah. Instead Islam awaits a Messiah it calls Al Mahid. Jesus, according Islamic teaching, will also appear to conquer and defeat all infidels and then destroy the power of the Cross and convert everyone to Islam.[5] Mart De Haan and Jimmy De Young who host the documentary, make little effort to discredit these claims that are so contrary to Christian teaching. In failing to do so, they create a false impression of kinship to Islam.

In an article entitled "Why is it Hard for Muslims to believe in Christ as their Saviour?" that RBC has published on its website as a resource to be read alongside the documentary, Dan Vander Lugt writes:

> When Muhammad observed the church and the "Christian" rulers of his day, he saw that they violated the very principles they claimed to uphold. Considering the flagrant corruption and idolatry of the Christian world, it isn't surprising that he and other early leaders of Islam assumed that every aspect of Christianity, including its Scriptures and key doctrines, was corrupt.

> As Muslim armies swept through "Christian" lands they found that they were often welcomed as liberators. The astonishing speed of their conquests, along with their conviction that they were restoring the pure monotheism of the Bible, gave them even more confidence that their mission was God-ordained and blessed.

> Early exposure to a debased Christianity was probably

enough by itself to thoroughly prejudice Muslims. But in a few centuries they were exposed to an even more perverse distortion of Christian faith: the Crusades. During the centuries of the Crusades, brutal "Christian" armies, often in contrast to more humane and merciful Muslim leaders like Saladin, committed barbaric atrocities on a vast scale. Tragically, these atrocities were committed in the name of Jesus Christ.[6]

While Vander Lugt provides an historical interpretation of the spread of Islam and a common viewpoint of the historical Church, he also commits what has become an acceptable apostasy: a narrow examination of the growth and spread of Islam, an examination that suggests the spread of Islam was blessed and ordained by God. With carefully placed quotation marks Vander Lugt implies that the atrocities committed by Christians in the Crusades were very un-"Christian," but stacks all the evidence against Christianity so as to leave a sour taste in the reader's mouth for the Church. As the article's title suggests, this is the point, to reveal how unfavourable Christianity looks to Muslims. The result of such writing, however, is that Islam squirms out of any rightful criticism for its role in the Crusades as all attention is turned to the evils of the Church. What remains is a one-sided, skewed dialogue. At very least, the evils of Islam are revisioned, historically, as a reaction to the terrors and injustices of the Christian faith, and therefore are considered lesser evils. At their worst the evils of Islam are to be blamed on Christians, and Islam should not be criticized, is not responsible for any wrongs it has done, and is, therefore, historically 'cleared.'

The Church, and Christians, must answer for the wrongs done in the past. Church doctrine clearly outlines what is evil and what is good, and a clear examination of historical events like the Crusades will reveal who was falsely acting in the name of Christ and when. Whether Muslim doctrine would name Islamic acts during the time of the Crusades as sinful or not, Islam must also be held accountable for its sins.

The church of which I am a member is a partner of RBC ministries. Mart De Haan and Jimmy De Young are some of my favourite program hosts to watch and listen to. Their faith and doctrine is true and correct and founded on Biblical teachings. Yet I cannot comprehend how such men are incapable of stating important facts: the god of Islam is Allah, that great and powerful Satanic desert deity and his prophet is Muhammad, lover of the Sword and hater of the Cross of Christ. The Muslim and Christian faiths share a hope in a Messiah, but those Messiahs could not be more different. Islam elevates Muhammad above Christ and makes Christ his subject. The idea that Christ would negate his ministry to the world by destroying the works of the Cross is an alarming teaching, completely opposed to the message of the Church.

Another great theologian, Peter Kreeft, whose *Handbook of Christian Apologetics* is one of the best books on Christian apologetics I have ever read, does everything he can to name the common ground Christians and Muslims share. His writing is positive and hopeful, and rightly longs for a day when Muslims and Christians are brothers and sisters because of faith in Christ. Kreeft points out that Christ is the key to brotherhood, but as he writes, he nearly turns "Christian" and "Muslim" into interchangeable terms so that the important distinction Christ makes is a mere aside, less important that the present illusion of oneness.

I am profoundly disturbed by these findings. Is it possible that the above men, great men of faith, are being misled as were some German theologians during the time of Hitler? Several well respected and influential theologians of Hitler's time believed that Hitler was working as the hand of God. The most well known of these scholars who fully supported Hitler and the Nazi regime was Gerhard Kittel whose other legacy was the massive ten volume *Theological Dictionary of the New Testament*. Kittel was one of the most brilliant Biblical scholars of the 20th Century in Germany and yet erroneously endorsed one of the most evil regimes the world has ever seen.

There is no question in my mind that Allah and Yaweh are on the opposite ends of the spiritual realm as are Muhammad and Jesus. To imply anything else is simply heresy. Kreeft writes,

> Christ... insists that "no one can come to the Father but by me." Whatever truth [Muhammad] taught Moslems about God is really present in Christ the Logos, the full revelation of God. If Moslems are saved, they are saved by Christ.... We cannot stop "proselytizing," for proselytizing means leading our brothers Home.

On this point Kreeft and I agree. For Christians to preach the Gospel we must recognize the difference between the gods, otherwise we have no real message to share. The Cross of Christ is the common ground on which all people are saved. He is the difference, and what a difference he makes!

WHAT IS TRUTH?

At the beginning of the first century AD, Pontius Pilate asked, "What is Truth?" when truth himself stood before him. His question was half-hearted, an aside, and the political figure then washed from his hands the culpability of that earth-shattering Truth. Are we, like Pilate, fickle with the facts?

Christ, truth incarnate, stated that, "Where two or three are gathered together in my name, there I am in their midst of them."[7] Does this statement still ring true? For it seems more likely that when two or three Christians are gathered there are two or three different opinions and points of view, mostly on issues that are not important. At least not important to the central theme of the Bible: the story of Redemption and mankind's only hope through the person of Jesus Christ.

Pierre Rehov, the French filmmaker, notes that:

> All Muslim believers believe that, ultimately, Islam will prevail on earth. They believe this is the only true religion and there is no room, in their mind, for interpretation. The main difference between moderate Muslims and extremists is that moderate Muslims don't think they will see the absolute victory of Islam during their life-time, therefore they respect other beliefs. The extremists believe that the fulfilment of the Prophecy of Islam and ruling the entire world as described in the [Quran], is for today. Each victory of Bin Laden convinces 20 million moderate Muslims to become extremists.... Every successful terror attack is considered a victory by the radical Islamists. Everywhere Islam expands there is regional conflict. Right now, there are thousands of candidates for martyrdom lining up in training camps in Bosnia, Afghanistan and Pakistan. Inside Europe, hundreds of illegal mosques are preparing the next step of brain washing to lost young men who cannot find a satisfying identity in the Occidental world. Israel is much more prepared for this than the rest of the world will ever be.

Yes, there will be more suicide killings in Europe and the U.S. Sadly, this is only the beginning.[8]

Where is the resolve and unity so apparent in the Muslim world among Christian believers? Christians face huge roadblocks, much because of fear, in progress toward the goal of their faith: the redemption of the world through their message about Christ. Pope Benedict's recent "apology" for a statement he made about Islam shows how strongly the Church and the West fears making any statement that could offend Muslims. Pope Benedict "apologized" to the Muslim world after he "enraged Muslims by quoting from a medieval text linking the spread of Islam to violence."[9]

Benedict quoted a conversation between 14th century Byzantine Christian Emperor Manuel Paleologos II and an educated Persian on the truths of Christianity and Islam:

> "The emperor comes to speak about the issue of jihad, holy war," the Pope said. "He said, I quote, 'Show me just what Muhammad brought that was new, and there you will find things only evil and inhuman, such as his command to spread by the sword the faith he preached.'"[10]

The Pope said he was "deeply sorry" for the strong reaction to his remarks in parts of the Muslim world: two churches in the West Bank were burned, and five others were hit with fire bombs and gunfire in response to the Pope's words, words he emphasized were a quote, not his personal thoughts.[11] Some newspapers speculated that the killing of Sister Leonella Sgorbati, a nun in her mid-sixties who served with the Missionaries of the Consolation in Mogadishu, Somalia, was a sign of

Somali Muslims' dissatisfaction with the Pope's words and his regret that fell short of an apology.[12]

Whether the Pope's regret was an actual apology or not, it is clear that for security reasons, the statement was required to alleviate violence and protest that raged in parts of the Muslim world. Police headquarters across Italy were ordered to raise security throughout the country at potential Catholic targets.[13] Ironically, the issue was not whether the quotation was true or not, but that it made Muslims, especially in Africa and the Middle East, angry. The Pope's apology shows he desired to stem violence, but also seems to emphasize the veracity of the quote.

Although the controversy and violence surrounding the Pope's speech suggests there is little room to publicly speak about Islam in any way other than Islam endorses, there is some evidence that there are people in and outside of the Muslim world who believe it is time for moderation and to champion free speech. While some Muslims suggest the Pope's comments might lead to war, others, the government of Turkey, for example, welcome him to his planned visit to the country.

There are signs of distress and promise in other parts of the world. When a Berlin opera house recently cancelled "Idomeneo," a famous Mozart work, because the German police were concerned a scene in which King Idomeneo is shown on stage with the severed heads of Buddha, Jesus, Muhammad and the sea god Poseidon[14] could enrage Muslims and pose a security risk, Chancellor Angela Merkel urged Germans not to bow to fears of Islamic violence. Interestingly, the opera was cancelled before anyone raised protest. Merkel stated publicly:

> "I think the cancellation was a mistake. I think self-censorship does not help us against people who want to practise violence in the name of Islam....It makes no sense to retreat."[15]

Other voices follow suit, warning "political correctness poses a threat to free expression for journalists, politicians, [academics],"[16] artists, and people of faith. Responding to the Berlin opera house's decision to cancel Mozart's famous work, Flemming Rose, culture editor of Denmark's *Jyllands-Posten*, which faced serious Muslim protest after publishing satirical cartoons of the Prophet Muhammad last year, said bowing to fears of violent Muslim reaction only worsens the problem:

> It's like deja vu...This is exactly the kind of self-censorship I and my newspaper have been warning against.... You play into the hands of the radicals. You are telling them: your tactics are working. This is a victory for the radicals. It's weakening the moderate Muslims who are our allies in this battle of ideas.[17]

The Vatican's handling of the Pope's speech, the cancellation of Mozart's opera, the furor over the publication of Muhammad's picture in a Danish editorial suggest that we in the West are afraid. We cannot live in fear. How we respond to threats or conflict with the Muslim world is telling. Moderate Muslims show reason and restraint while many radicals send a clear message: don't dare to say anything about Islam that we might find unfavorable, whether it is historical, factual, or not.

Christians should take note of the courage and intelligence of Angela Merkel and Flemming Rose; furthermore, Christians should note the passion and unity of Muslims. As Christians, it is time for us to declare war, but we must not fight with the violence or fear that exists in much of the Muslim world. We must wage a war of the heart, a war against our true enemy: the Enemy of souls who seeks to kill, steal, and destroy. Christian doctrine emphasizes that the war to be waged is not against flesh and blood[18], but against a very real evil that fights in the world.

We must fight with truth, light, and with love. The question is, how do Christians live out these principles in the world in which they live, with an often volatile, political landscape? And further, how do Christians act in the physical realm where conflict is resolved not only with logic, laws, and ideas, but, when push comes to shove, with swords and guns and bombs? .

HARD-LINE SUGGESTIONS IN A SOFT, POLITICALLY CORRECT LANDSCAPE

There are a number of obstacles that the West and especially Christians face: political correctness, an over-realized sense of tolerance, and violence that threatens. How should the Western World respond to the new world war? If it continues to delicately walk around issues in the pretext of political-correctness and a false sense of multiculturalism and religious freedom I fear the years ahead will result in many more human tragedies to a cruel enemy.

THE EXAMPLE OF ISRAEL AND HEZBOLLAH

The conflict we have faced and will face is complicated and unique. The recent armed conflict between Israel and Hezbollah is a signpost of the new territory that Islam and the non-Muslim world occupy. As Hezbollah launched rockets into Israel, threatening and claiming the lives of civilians, Israel retaliated with force, and the almost unanimous call from European countries was for a ceasefire. Wrongs were clearly committed by both sides. However, United Nations Secretary General Kofi Annan strongly suggested Israel committed war crimes. In the international media crisis that ensued what often seemed to be lost in the crossfire of debate was the fact that an Islamic terrorist organization was waging war against an entire country and hiding in a neighbouring state like a virus.

The call from Lebanese Prime Minister Fuad Siniora for a ceasefire was completely understandable, as he saw his country ravaged and innocents die. Yet what was Israel to do? It was thrown into a conflict it wanted no part of and its security as a nation was at risk as Hezbollah missiles became more accurate and reached further into Israel. From a long-term perspective, the best action for Israel was to eradicate the terrorist organization whose mandate includes seeing the end of Israel as a nation. From a security standpoint, the best option for Israel was to wipe out the terrorists at the time, rather than face another conflict five or ten years down the road when Hezbollah regroups and re-arms. Israel's position and security seemed a rare topic in media coverage.

THE EXAMPLE OF GUANTANAMO BAY

It is admirable that people do not want war, do not want to see Israelis fighting against Palestinians. It is also appropriate that people are repelled by the possibility of torture and mistreatment of prisoners which has been another issue of hot debate in North America and around the world. There seems, however, to be a present day tendency to jump on a bandwagon of ideals but not consider facts carefully. To me, the United States' military prison at Guantanamo Bay exemplifies the tendency for people to champion an ideal without contextualizing the issue at hand. If there was an idea that was right but made wrong it is Guantanamo Bay. In the new world war the rules of engagement are not yet understood. Terrible rumours of torture at the US Naval base where terrorist suspects are held are being investigated and the there is much concern about the rights of prisoners. Although the possibility of torture must be addressed, there are other factors at work that are making the war against Islamic terror more difficult to wage.

Beyond reports of injustice to prisoners, the media also reports that some detainees held at Guantanamo Bay obstinately hold to plans of jihad. They admit without fear that upon their release they will continue their unrelenting attack against innocents in brutal and savage ways. Let us remember that whereas these prisoners are allowed unbelievable rights, Western prisoners caught by Muslims are not offered the same rights. Torture, mutilation and beheading are the things reserved for those that fight on the side of "Human Freedom." Yet because of instances of torture by US troops to prisoners, which are intolerable and must be judged justly, people only criticize the prison.

No matter how the enemy treats us, we must live by our principles and international law, never stooping to the level of those who would violate human rights and grossly harm our soldiers. With those principles in mind, how should Guantanamo Bay and prisoners in other Western jails be treated? Humanely but severely. Should those considered dangerous to society be given the very literature used as inspiration for their acts of terror? Nazi prisoners in Allied jails were not dressed in their uniforms or given *Mein Kampf* to read. The idea is ridiculous and yet Muslim prisoners demand to be allowed a copy of the Quran. It is not inhumane or hypocritical to deny a prisoner their religious texts, even in a society that values the freedom of religion. The right of prisoners to read their religious documents should be suspended until, at a case by case level, it can be determined that they will not use the same literature as inspiration for the violent acts many prisoners promise to commit against innocents upon their release.

Overcoming the Roadblocks

There are some things Christians and non-Christians agree upon in Western society. We capture and punish those in our societies who carry out evil and harm. Paedophiles are sought out and hunted by security forces. Murderers are placed on wanted posters until captured. Thieves that break into our homes and steal our goods do not receive a free pass once caught. Rapists often receive severe consequences and jail time when convicted of their offences. Few people, whether Liberal or Conservative-aligned disagree with the consequences handed by the state to those who harm innocents.

We tend to agree that those who plan or practice paedophilia, murder, thievery and rape should be closely monitored and kept from accomplishing their evil schemes. So what about those who mean to enact terrorism?

CSIS has stated that there are 50 terrorist groups operating in Canada. These must all be identified, exposed and eliminated. There should be no question that jail time and deportation are the consequences for anyone who proves to be a threat. A discussion and clear outline for what the state considers an organization aligned with the spirit of Islamic terrorism should exist. Such a discussion and a set of standards would free non-Muslims from fear and free peaceful Muslims from criticism and suspicion.

Speaking of the United States, Brigitte Gabriel argues that the government needs to take stronger action individuals who seek to destroy Western culture with violence as well as individuals who impede the fight of the war on terrorism. She suggests the implementation of the following initiatives for American homeland security:

- Closed borders

- Reform of the Immigration and Naturalization service (INS)
- Increased human intelligence
- Profile, Profile and Profile
- Control education of foreign students of hostile countries
- Develop alternative energy sources
- Silence any teaching of hate and intolerance against the USA[19]

Though her suggestions may seem extreme to some, Gabriel speaks from the experience of witnessing her home country of Lebanon, which she recalls was once the "Paris of the Middle East," ruined by terrorists. Referring to the United States, Gabriel concludes that "Our willingness as a nation to support our intelligence community and provide them with whatever laws that will enable them to track and infiltrate cells in America will determine our demise or survival. The tragedy of 11 September 2001 could be the end of terrorism on American soil or the beginning of the end of American civilization."

In my mind, there is no question that there needs to be transparency from and public scrutiny in Mosques. Words taught and spoken in official gatherings should be recorded and available to the public. Mosques with any association or sympathy to terrorist cells must be investigated by public officials who are appointed by the government. Gabriel insists that mosques around the world are a part of the problem instead of being a part of the solution. A recent report by Freedom House/Center For Religious Freedom clearly reveals the toxic flow of religious hatred that Saudi Arabia especially has unleashed in the United States:

> The center studied over 200 books and publications col-
> lected from more than a dozen of the most prominent
> mosques and Islamic institutions in the United States,
> including those in Washington, DC, New York, Chicago,

Houston, Dallas, Los Angeles and Oakland. All of these
books and publications were financed and produced directly or indirectly by the Saudi government. Some of
the books were texts from Islamic schools. Some were
publications issued by the Saudi government specifically
to provide guidance to Muslims living in or visiting the
United States.

In their relations with all non-Muslims, these Saudi
books and publications repeatedly exhort Muslims to
"hate them for their religion,"- meaning us infidels - to
"hate for Allah's sake...always oppose them in every
way," maintain a "wall of resentment" against them. They
say that Democracy is "responsible for all of the horrible
wars" of the 20th Century and that "attractive names like
democracy, justice, freedom, brotherhood and equality"
cause all of the world's problems. [20]

The literature also asserts that all religions but Islam are false, and
that it is the religious duty of every Muslim to impose "functionally
Islamic governments" in every country in the world.

This religious duty is "binding in principle, in law, in
self-defense, in community, and as a sacred obligation of
jihad." In order to fulfill this "sacred obligation of jihad",
they must invade its Western heartland, and struggle to
overcome it until all the world shouts by the name of the
Prophet [Muhammad] and the teachings of Islam spread
throughout the world. Only then will Muslims achieve

their fundamental goal… All religion will be exclusively for Allah.[21]

This type of education presents a major problem when we think about stemming the radicalism in Muslim communities.

A secure forum should be created where open debates between Muslim scholars and non-Muslims can occur. Furthermore, Islamic schools in the West should be openly observed and lessons from the Quran in Arabic must be followed by translation into English. Any teaching that is deemed sympathetic to terrorist behaviour should be denounced and guilty parties should be held accountable in the same way teachers who have taught false things about the Holocaust have been held accountable in our society.

A FOOTNOTE TO CHRISTIANS

Christians must offer the Gospel of Christ to all people including Muslims, many of whom are anxious to hear and receive it. As Christians we are always told by the Scriptures to give an account of the hope that we have within us. Can Muslims be our friends and partners in our free and Democratic cultures? They can and are! But in so doing they must always be able to answer and give an account of what they believe. Most of all, their actions must prove coherent in regards to their stance against terrorism and their lives must prove unquestioned loyalty to the country in which they reside. Anything in their lives that would support Islamic terrorism is to be considered an act of treason.

As Christians have in the past, so can we today lead in an example of godliness, showing respect and loyalty to our country and adhere without wavering to the Scripture's high call of love, obedience, and integrity.

Chapter Eleven: The End of Things

He who has an ear, let him hear

— Revelation 3:6

In my original research, I did not anticipate the following topic. Since I sat down to write this book, my research has taken me down some interesting roads with surprising twists and turns. Current events reported in all different forms of media have compelled and directed me down a path toward the following discussion. Previously, I was not aware of Islam's view of the end times, and was surprised to once again see that Islam's writings on the subject are a clear revision of Christianity's eschatological predictions.

At the beginning of the book, I highlighted that humanity lives against the backdrop of a spiritual war, an ongoing battle between forces of good and evil, God and Satan. That is the script. Hopefully all will choose a side and learn the way of spiritual warfare. Nevertheless, all people, whether they are aware of it or not, or whether they like it or not, play a role. Real, physical warfare is a reality in the battle. Guns are fired, swords are drawn, words are shared. However the battle takes place, it fits under a greater banner of spiritual good or evil, for, the ultimate fight is a spiritual one.

The Bible predicts the end of the battle between Good and Evil, when God will bring the fullness of his kingdom to a new heaven and new earth and once for all deal with Evil. Death will be defeated, and those who believe in Christ will live forever in peace. The book of Revelation tells the story in symbolic language. Though the timeline of the prophecy and how events will come about in history are obscure and disputed, the basic message of the book is clear: Jesus is victorious and will defeat all evil; those who trust in him, though they will experience suffering on earth, will ultimately be redeemed and live with God in heaven where they will never suffer again. This message has encouraged Christian believers since the first century, and motivated believers to wait patiently and, in the meantime, live good lives on earth.

Many other religions have different views of life on earth, the "goal" of history, and the afterlife. I believe the Bible's perspective on history and reality to be true, but admit I believe these things in faith, and that all people should have the freedom to choose what they will believe. I must, however, admit alarm that Islam has rewritten Christianity's script and its prediction of the final outcome of world events.

My alarm is grounded in the very words of the script I hold in my hand. The apostle John, at the end of Revelation writes:

> *I warn everyone who hears the word of the prophecy of this book: if anyone adds anything to them, God will add to him the plagues described in this book. And if anyone takes away from this book of prophecy, God will take away from him his share in the tree of life and in the holy city, which are described in this book.*[1]

John's concluding statement is a bold one to be sure. However, if his words were truly God-inspired then they are necessary: a protection against those who would revise God's word about the end of time and therefore potentially manipulate readers. Truly the fear of death and what awaits the dead can and does motivate the way people live their lives. We have already discussed how many Muslims are willing to take their lives and kill others in hopes of attaining a favourable eternal life. The Apostle John's writings are clear: as Christians anticipate the fullness of God's kingdom, they are to love their enemies, embrace suffering so that the Gospel can impact more lives, and be unafraid of death, for the hope of eternal life awaits them. John's message has empowered thousands of Christian believers to embrace true martyrdom.

How are Christian martyrdom and Muslim martyrdom different? Chesterton answers the question for us, underlining the difference between dying at the hand of others because of faith, and killing yourself and others:

> Obviously a suicide is the opposite of a martyr. A martyr is a man who cares so much for something outside him, that he forgets his own personal life. A suicide is a man who cares so little for anything outside him, that he wants to see the last of everything. One wants something to begin: the other wants everything to end. In other words, the martyr is noble, exactly because (however he renounces the world or execrates all humanity) he confesses this ultimate link with life; he sets his heart outside himself: he dies that something may live. The suicide is ignoble because he has not this link with being: he is a mere destroyer: spiritually, he destroys the universe.[2]

The Christian view of the end times is as different from the Muslim view as Christian martyrs are different from Muslim martyrs. Yahiya Emerick explains the Muslim view of the end times, which gives insight into the ongoing Islamic terrorism and warfare around the world. Clearly, the Muslim and Christian interpretation of the end times and the believer's role in seeing the goal of history realized is opposite. Where the Christian is called to further a spiritual kingdom that rules the heart and calls non-believers to submission through repentance, the Muslim is called to spread a kingdom where non-believers submit or die. Like Christianity, Islam anticipates an Antichrist. Emerick identifies the Antichrist as 'Dajjal'.

> Before the Dajjal appears, though, a great Muslim leader will arise who will unify all faithful Muslims under his

banner and will wage many successful campaigns against
the enemy of Islam. This leader's title is the Mahdi.
Muslims look forward to his appearance and expect that
many victories in Palestine and India will be achieved.
Invading armies from Europe will be vanquished as well.
After conquering the Middle East, peace and prosperity
will fill the Earth, and economic benefits will be overwhelming. The main block of Muslim forces will then
retire to Palestine when rumors about the appearance of
the Dajjal will begin to circulate among the people.... He
will amass a military might, which he will use to harass
and destroy all vestiges of true religious expression.

The reign of the Dajjal will last for 40 days...he will even
try to invade the city of Medina in Arabia...battles will
rage for several days, with Muslim soldiers taking heavy
casualties. When all appears lost... a rumor of deliver-
ance spreads like wildfire and a voice will be heard saying, 'the one who listens to your pleas has come'.

When the time for the morning payer arrives, the Prophet
Jesus, who had been saved from dying on the cross thousands of years before and had been kept in Paradise by
God, will descend in the midst of Damascus. After join-
ing the Muslims in prayer, he will lead the Mahdi's forces
against the Dajjal's army... Jesus will strike down the
Dajjal with a lance, and his reign of tyranny will be over.[3]

According to the sayings of the prophet Muhammad, Jesus will speak
to Christians and Jews of the world and convert them to Islam. He will

succeed in breaking the worship of the cross. Jesus will live a normal life on earth, he will marry and have children and live for only 40 more years – the rest of his natural life span.

The writings of Turkish Grandsheikh, Nazim Adil al-Haqqani, help us further understand the Islamic view of the end times:

> We know that the world is being prepared for huge appearances. In a short time there will be a common change, physically then spiritually. Time is now over. All nations and all mankind are being prepared for something that is approaching soon. These are huge events, unexpected huge events.

> I am knowing and you must believe that I have come on the order of Divine Will. I have come on the command of the Sal (Prophet) and of the saints. I have not come to this place but to make Haq (truth) to be like the bright light of the sun.

The Turkish Grandsheikh explains that:

> As believers of traditions, we believe in a saviour who will come first, before Jesus Christ. We have in our traditions his name, which is Muhammad d'ul Mahdi. He is coming, but his arrival [will] be after a great war. It will be a fight with big powers with each other. And in that war the saviour will come like a divine hand from the heavens to the earth and stop the war.

After a short time a tyrant will appear, well known through traditions as the Anti-Christ. When Jesus Christ was on the earth he never touched a sword, but now he is coming as a saviour. In his time all technology will be finished.... These will be very difficult days for mankind. There will be strong fighting. Very many people will be killed.

Then the Lord will command Al-Mahdi Alaihi As Salam to appear. Now he is in a cave, in a big, deep cave. No one can approach it. Jinns (angels) are protecting and guarding him. When he comes, he will say, *Allahu, Akbar Allahu, Akbar Allahu, Akbar* (Allah is the Greatest) and this will be heard from the East to the West without a doubt.[4]

The passages have some striking similarities to Biblical writing:

And I saw an angel coming down out of heaven, having the key to the Abyss and holding in his hand a great chain. He seized the dragon, the ancient serpent, who is the devil, or Satan, and bound him for a thousand years. He threw him into the Abyss, and locked and sealed it over him, to keep from deceiving the nations anymore until the thousand years were ended.

After that he must be set free for a short time.... When the thousand years are over, Satan will be released from prison and will go out to deceive the nations in the four corners of the earth—Gog and Magog[5]—to gather them for battle. In

131

number they are like the sand of the seashore. They marched across the breadth of the earth and surrounded the camp of God's people, the city he loves.

But fire came down from heaven and devoured them. And the devil who deceived them, was thrown into the lake of burning sulphur, where the Beast and the False prophet[6] had been thrown. They will be tormented day and night for ever and ever.[7]

I am not scholar of the end times, but I do note some interesting parallels and Islamic revisions of Christian writing that are to me, in a word, frightening. Islamic writing and teaching awaits a final saviour who will declare the greatness of Allah. He is hidden, waiting in a deep cave. Christian writing suggests something other than a saviour lies waiting in that cave, it is no saviour, but the final enemy of God awaiting release to deceive and destroy the world. The Christian hope is that he will not be victorious, but will be defeated by God and removed along with his false religion, forever, from the world.

If the words of the Bible are true, then Islam, as we see in the above passages, has set itself as an enemy of God. It is aligned, like many other religions and movements throughout history, with false religion that, ultimately, will be judged.

Perhaps it is on this note that I should end. The question for me is no longer, *Are we at War,* but *How will we fight?* I, for one, do not want to be unaware of the enemy's schemes. Ultimately, I do not believe that Muslim people are the enemy. I do not want to see Muslims dead or dying in the streets; I long to see them set free. From religious leaders who hold them in the grip of a cruel religion. Free from hopelessness, violence, and fear. Free from oppression that denies so many of its adherents, especially women, basic freedoms so many in the world enjoy today.

Although Muslim people are not the enemy, many are a real, physical threat to the security we desire, and the freedom so many have fought for in the world. Muslim men and women daily strap bombs to their bodies, hit the streets, and kill innocent people, both Muslim and non-Muslim for the sake of Allah, in hatred of democracy, Israel, and all other Infidels. They live under a veil of deception.

At the beginning of the book I suggested that, perhaps, we will be forced to sharpen our swords; forced to fight. I believe there is room to roll up our sleeves and to land physical blows in self defence, to protect countless innocents from further harm. Ultimately, though physical acts of self defence might be necessary, they are not the solution. Beyond the sword, there is another object to raise, high as the heavens for all to see. For us, it is the Gospel of Christ and the message of his life. The wisdom of the Cross is the only message that can bring lasting peace for it can free people from the powerful deception ingrained in their minds and teach a more excellent way to live.

Conclusion

I have never written a book. If I am honest, part of me desires the former illusion that covered my now shattered vision of the world. For me, writing and research was a difficult journey laden with pain. For, I see a mad religion making a broken world more mad. I look to the past and remember the horrors committed by evil powers in my own lifetime; I look to the present and see similar atrocities committed daily throughout the world. As I write, I am compelled to ask, *What will the future hold?* I consider Holland, the country of my birth, and my heart breaks to see new cuts spill blood from the scars of old wounds. My reaction to the facts before me are as complicated as the history of our world: anger and hatred at the mention of just one murder or rape in the name of Allah; compassion for millions in a sea of faces held captive by a religion which on the outside has the appearance of beauty, but inside is full of the bones of the dead; hope for the world, and yet fear.

And still in my mind I cannot erase the image of the Sword of Islam raising itself to the Cross of Christ. When I see it, the bittersweet picture of the Cross outweighs my fear and gives hope, for, I remember that where the Sword raped, tortured, murdered and enslaved, the Cross healed and restored. And on that Cross I see the clearest picture of total submission that ever revealed itself to the world.

CHAPTER TWELVE:
SHARIA FINANCE AND BEYOND

*and [they] deceived and Allah deceived and Allah
is the best of deceivers*

— Sura 3:54

While the world watched with keen interest at the historic election of Barack Hussein Obama to the presidency of the United States, the financial system in the United States and around the world was being turned on its head. As the operator of an insurance and financial planning agency I was acutely aware of the shockwaves sent through the financial sector.

Throughout the presidential election there was much talk about the role of the mainstream media and it's stance toward candidates. Oftentimes, the things average North Americans are interested in or want to hear are not reported by such media outlets. Because of their silence on many things, I have made it a personal habit not to depend on mainstream media outlets for information. I visit and seek out websites and other media outlets who do not shy away from newsworthy stories about the Islamic world, however controversial the truth of the stories may seem.

During the conference I attended in Ontario, Sam Solomon gave a dire warning about the marriage of Sharia finance into our existing financial institutions. When, a month after the conference our financial institutions crashed and I learned AIG, the global financier, had been rescued by government funds and was now accepting Sharia finances as part of its bailout, I was alarmed.

Perhaps an unfamiliar concept to many, Sharia finance, as explained by the prominent terrorism advocate Yousuf al-Qaradawi is "jihad with money."[1] You can imagine my surprise, then, when I learned about a closed meeting that brought together key figures of the United States Treasury Department and leading Sharia financers, a meeting that went virtually unreported in the mainstream news media. The seminar was entitled "Islamic Finance 101." Held in November of 2008 its purpose was to provide Treasury regulators with information about Islamic Finance.

Alex Alexiev, Vice President for Research for the Center for Security Policy and author, whose current research focuses on issues related to Islamic extremism and terrorism, reports:

> Not surprisingly, the picture of Sharia finance that emerged from the presentations … was that of a God-ordained, socially-conscious, morally superior and more profitable financial system that's ready to replace its failed capitalist counterpart. And, as if to make this picture even more idyllic and persuasive, the seminar was introduced by none other than the administrator of the $700 billion in government handouts to our currently nationalized banking system, Neel Kashkari.[2]

What shocked me most was to learn that in the recent past the Treasury Department shut down Sharia banks because of proof that they financed terrorism. Truly the financial crisis is turning many things upside down, including prudent and good governance. Alexiev concludes in his important article that the United States Government's participation in such a seminar was more than unconscionable, but a "dereliction of duty"[3] for it purported to provide regulators with reliable information on Islamic finance, but did not invite critics of Sharia finance to attend, featured key figures of the Sharia financial system with known ties to terrorism and corruption, and overlooked the history of Sharia's jihad through finance. In a chilling statement Alexiev writes, "It is essential to understand here that Sharia law is an immutable and indivisible doctrine that regulates each and every aspect of a Muslim's life and, unless you believe in all of it, you are an apostate and subject to death."[4]

Why do such statements get little attention in the mainstream public discourse? And why do we fail to see the unabashed efforts of certain Muslims to change the Western way of life into an Islamic one?

I am concerned, in particular, for the upcoming generation, for my grandchildren. With much rhetoric being thrown about announcing hope and a new way of engaging the world, and as young people all over the world are energized by the Obama zeitgeist, I believe we must be more cautious than ever about prevailing threats. And as we look to the future and build bridges, we must not forget either the past or the times. Andrew McCarthy, a contributing editor to the *National Review Online* writes:

> There is nothing less civilized than rewarding evil and thus guaranteeing more of it. High-minded as it is commonly made to sound, it is not civilized to appease evil, to treat it with "dignity and respect," to rationalize its root causes, to equivocate about whether evil really is evil, and, when all else fails, to ignore it — to purge the very mention of its name — in the vain hope that it will just go away. Evil doesn't do nuance. It finds you, it tests you, and you either fight it or you're part of the problem. [5]

McCarthy reminds us that America is the world's most generous nation, dispensing $21 billion dollars in foreign aid, annually, a figure that does not include emergency military expeditions or aid to victims of earthquakes, other natural disasters, or wars. He notes, also, that Obama's signature legislative proposal during his short time in the Senate, which did not pass into law, was the Global Poverty Bill, a trillion-dollar redistribution of wealth from the American taxpayer to the international community. McCarthy seems to scratch his head at the thought of the renewed efforts the American people are making to reach out to the world: "George W. Bush freed 50 million Muslims from tyranny and gave them a chance to make better lives even as the rigors of doing so devoured his presidency — all the while launching, for Africa, the most generously funded program for AIDS prevention and treatment in history" and yet Obama recently "bleated across Europe that America has been 'arrogant.' By his lights, our actions since 9/11 (which include writing constitutions for Iraq and Afghanistan that enshrined Sharia, the Muslim legal code, as governing law) have suggested we are 'at war with Islam.'"[6]

So, when I hear young people summarize the threat and terror of radical Islam as an understandable response to Western sins I fear for their future.

SOCIAL JUSTICE VIA THE ZEITGEIST

A few months ago I wrote a letter to the local newspaper that put into question the Liberal Party of Canada's demands for the release of Omar Khadr from Guantanamo Bay, an imprisonment their very own party endorsed when in power in the days and months after 9/11. Media outlets in Canada had been playing select portions of Khadr's taped interrogations as a 15 year old as proof of his torture. At the time I wrote the letter Khadr was 22, in US custody for seven years. Hailed as a child soldier unjustly held against his will, the media's focus in recent months has been on the injustice of Khadr's plight, and often overlooks the fact that the grenade he allegedly threw on an Afghani road killed a US Marine.

After being back for only a couple of days from the conference in Ontario featuring Sam Solomon, I received an email that was sent to everyone in my church body, rallying members of the congregation to attend a public protest at Kings University College in Edmonton with the hopes of bringing 5000 people together to demand the release of Omar Khadr. Surprised, I started to look into the matter and soon discovered that the rally was part of a fairly long and detailed effort by certain students and instructors at the Christian University. The endeavor was presented as an expression of acquiring justice for a child soldier.

As a concerned citizen and Christian I had some conversations with leaders at Kings College, and soon realized the substantial amount of emotional energy as well as financial resources that were being used to secure Khadr's release. In February of 2009 the University was featured on CBC, Canada's national news broadcast. Along with three Members of Parliament from the Liberal party, Muslim clerics and the student body, the leadership of Kings College announced that it had agreed to work together with these entities to secure Khadr's release and help reintegrate him back into Canadian society. The University developed a home schooling curriculum it will fund and provide Khadr once he is released.

Kings University College is not only supported by, but belongs to my church denomination. As a Christian I certainly stand for and believe in mercy and justice. But I would be remiss if I failed to mention how the blood seemed to drain from my body when I learned just how committed the school was to this issue of "social justice." In conversation with the leadership of Kings, I highlighted what to me was the tragic irony of how my own denomination and church body was caught up in the politically correct drama of freeing a known terrorist. I suggested to the leadership they focus efforts to work with the government and media to secure the release of Amanda Lindhout, the young Albertan journalist held hostage in Somalia by Muslim terrorists, held unjustly for ransom, but to no avail. For some reason Omar Khadr is the poster child for the

University's social conscience. A conscience perhaps in touch with the current zeitgeist, but one I believe is desperately out of touch.

DECEPTION ROBED IN POLITICAL CORRECTNESS

I was concerned that my entire church body received an email urging people to champion the release of an alleged Islamic militant. Soon after the incident, a friend at the church, aware of my research into Islam, approached me and asked if I knew about a brochure posted on the church's bulletin board. The brochure announced a religious conference at the Red Deer College called "Life After Death, Myth or Reality?" organized by the Ahmadiyya Muslim Community, and inviting Christians to attend. The Ahmadiyya's described themselves as follows:

> This is a religious organization, with branches in over
> 185 Countries. This is the most dynamic denomination
> of Islam in modern history, with membership exceeding
> millions. The Ahmadiyya community was established in
> 1889 by Hadhrat Mirza Ghulam Ahmad (1835-1908).
> He claimed to be the expected reformer of the latter
> days. The Community he started is an embodiment
> of the benevolent message of Islam – Peace, universal
> brotherhood, and submission to the will of God – in
> its pristine purity. Wherever the Community is estab-
> lished, it endeavours to exert a constructive influence of
> Islam, through social projects, educational institutes,
> health services, Islamic publications, and construction
> of Mosques, despite being bitterly persecuted in some
> countries. Amadhi Muslims have earned the distinction

of being a law abiding, peaceful, persevering and be-
nevolent community. It encourages interfaith dialogue,
and diligently defends Islam and tries to correct mis-
understandings about Islam in the West. It advocates
peace, tolerance, love and understanding among followers of different faiths. It's present Head, Hadhrat Mirza
Masroor Ahmad was elected in 2003.

The brochure concluded with the following statement in bolded typeface:
LOVE FOR ALL HATRED FOR NONE. Upon further research,
I discovered that the brochure left out a few details. What it did not
include was that the Ahmadiyya founder Ahmad also claimed that he
was the second coming of Christ and that Jesus survived the crucifixion
and later died a normal death. Further, he taught, as does the Qur'an,
that when the Muslim Messiah comes, the power of the cross will be
broken.

I found myself seated in the Red Deer College conference at the back
of the theatre. The presenters were scholars from Buddhism, Christianity,
Judaism, Aboriginal and Islamic faiths. The Ahmiddya sect, however
was running the show. As the presenters were close to being seated, I
overheard a couple of college students behind me discuss the course on
religion they were taking. As they bantered back and forth they ridiculed
the Christian faith and discussed their conviction that Jesus was never
crucified but escaped to India where he lived to the ripe old age of 125
years old. As we waited for the presentation to begin, the two students
also commented on the complete sensibility of Islam, in their opinion the
only religion that really "makes sense."

The presentations made by the member of each faith were, for the
most part inconsequential, but I waited with keen interest to hear the
final presenter Naseem Mehdi, who would discuss Islam. Mehdi, a

graduate from a Pakistani Islamic university, was touted as an expert in comparative studies of religions and Arabic. He also has a PHD in botany and is a recipient of the Governor General's Award for community service.

Mehdi's presentation was engaging. He spoke and carried himself with an air of familiarity, like a favorite uncle. His jokes were funny and his explanation of Islam appealing. I enjoyed his presentation! But I had, of course, major questions, which I was led to believe I could ask as a curious participant at the end of his speech. The questions, however, had to be hand written on cards that were then submitted to the moderator of the panel.

I quickly realized the entire evening, from start to finish, was a well choreographed attempt to promote the Ahmiddya's vision of Islam – palatable propaganda – with no room for real questions or debate. Since the evening was billed as a discussion of life and death, I wanted to ask Mehdi about the Islamic position on the afterlife and the black-faced blue-eyed angels Nakir and Munkir who, according to Islamic teaching, encounter people at their deaths. All questions, however, were picked up by the Ahmiddya's helpers and my honest questions were not asked of the panel. In the end we were fed milk toast, and there were no questions asked that hinted at or addressed any controversy concerning Islam.

After the presentation my wife and I went home. I sat in stunned silence for well over an hour digesting what had just occurred. It was by far one of the smoothest con jobs I had ever witnessed. I could completely understand why so many young college students in the audience were taken in and mesmerized. Without my in-depth research and understanding of Islam, Mehdi with his smooth and beautiful speech, would have had me too! With skill and finesse Mehdi shared an Islam of non-violence and peace, alluring and with no hint of violence toward or against Western values. To be honest, I was prepared to face a ranting imam. I was not ready for a convincing presentation that skillfully stepped around any mention of what Islam teaches and believes. Nor did I expect the seminar organizers to be handsome, highly educated men dressed in nice suits, offering a delicious spread of fine food and drink for those who were kind enough to attend.

As I sat in reflection, trying to come to terms with an Islam I may have unfairly judged, my wife helped me to unveil the glossy deception. She told me that in a break during the presentation, she left the theatre in search of a Diet Coke and walked by a small area that had been set aside, cordoned off by a large curtain. Behind the curtain was a small gathering of about ten women, all dressed from head to toe in dark robes, faces poking out from head-coverings. These were the wives of the Ahmaddiyas. Hidden away from the main event, sequestered and separate from the rest of us, shrouded in the clothing their religion designates their gender. Their secret presence was all the proof I needed that however convincing and enticing Mehdi and his cohorts were, like their women, his whole teaching was robed in lies and deception.

CHAPTER THIRTEEN: I SEE PICTURES

By this the children of God and the children of the devil are obvious: anyone who does not practice righteousness is not of God... He who does not love abides in death

— 1 John 3: 10-14

O Lord, perish the Jews and the Christians.... There shall be no two faiths in Arabia

— last words uttered by Mohammad while he lay dying

Earlier in the book I relayed some of my experience as a young boy in Holland. The horrors of World War II were great, destroying countless lives. My own family suffered during the war, but our suffering paled in comparison to many millions who were exterminated at the behest of evil men who, according to the belief system they held to so tightly, justified the deaths of an entire segment of society. More than six million Jews were murdered. My mind still reels with shock at such a statistic.

Time does not heal all wounds, nor does it eradicate hatred. Dangerous beliefs destructive to all of society do not simply disappear when the believer moves to a new country, changes his passport, and settles into a new way of life. I learned this lesson in the small town of Bentley, Alberta.

A mechanic in my small town, was at one point a high school teacher and the mayor of another small community nearby. A loving family man, in the course of his teaching career it was discovered that he was a Holocaust denier and had taught the belief to his students. The demise of his career became renowned worldwide as the media focused its attention on this small-town man who would not relent a despicable belief. As a result, he was fired from his job and, I think rightly, relegated to the fringes of society.

I remember our pastor at the time explaining to some of us men in the church that sometimes a person could be an overall decent human being but maintain an indefensible and illogical position on a certain issue and that reason, logic, or common sense debate could not change the person. The belief was so strongly embedded in their psyche, it was rather like having a mental illness. The man, however, still had to earn a living and he did so as a mechanic. He was good at his work and charged a very fair price for the work, which he always guaranteed. So, I would take my vehicle to him as needed. Wisdom dictated that we never discussed his views and he never offered to. The only person who paid a price for the senseless logic was the man himself, and so it should be.

To me, the scenario illustrates how society can effectively quell terrible beliefs while giving people the freedom to believe them. The man could still live, and live with his wrong belief, but society protected itself from those beliefs by marginalizing him and emphatically and intentionally agreeing that those beliefs were, in fact, wrong.

THE BRAVE NEW WORLD OF POLITICALLY CORRECT LUNACY

Now, however, in our brave new world of politically-correct lunacy, society seems unable to denounce such beliefs. In a stunning decision in Holland, a Dutch court charged Geert Wilders, a Member of Parliament, with hate speech for comments he made publicly about Islam, saying "in a democratic system, hate speech is considered so serious that it is in the general interest to …draw a clear line."[1] The court charged Wilders with the crime, citing that Wilder's "one-sided generalizations" went beyond the normal leeway his role as a politician allows. Some of his anti-Islamic statements included calling the Q'uran a fascist book and comparing it to Hitler's *Mein Kampf*. Wilders was already in the international spotlight for *Fitna*, his film that juxtaposed verses from the Quran against violent scenes and images of terrorism by radical Muslims. [2] In what is considered to be the most progressive country in Europe, Wilders says he has witnessed the unchecked growth of Islamofacism. In response to the lawsuit, Wilders has announced that the charges are an outright attack on freedom of speech.[3]

Wilder's, in his film, shows pictures of Muslim demonstrators holding up placards saying "God bless Hitler" and "Freedom go to hell."[4] It is a generalization to say all Muslims feel the same, but Wilders has evidence that some do. The clear line the courts seem to be drawing is one that carves a thick and deadly mark through freedom of speech and the frightening truth. In the court's opinion it is better to punish and marginalize a citizen for sounding the alarm about a dangerous segment of society than to marginalize and denounce the danger itself. While Muslim groups have celebrated the court action for defending Islam and any comparison made between it and the extremism of Nazism, Wilders is a virtual prisoner in his own home, threatened 24 hours a day because of a fatwa issued against his life. Wilders has had police protection since Dutch film director Theo van Gogh was killed by a radical Muslim in 2004.

Tragically, Wilder's experience is only one in a greater narrative, one plot line that reveals just how delicately the fate of Europe hangs in the balance. He is one more voice that the armies of political correctness mean to silence, one that the hordes of radical Islamists want to quash. Wilders joins the ranks of other politicians, like Pim Fortuyn and Ayaan Hirsi Ali and voices of free speech like Theo van Gogh, who were marginalized, and threatened, and tragically, in the case of Fortuyn and van Gogh, murdered for sounding the alarm.

Freedom of religion is a right provided to us as North Americans as part of the Canadian Charter of Rights and Freedoms and the Constitution of the United States. And throughout the rest of the western world citizens are guaranteed the right to religion and free speech. We must be on our guard. In Great Britain church bells are drowned out by the haunting sound of the Muslim call to prayer from minaret towers that dominate the country's skyline. The nation that produced Winston Churchill, one of greatest defenders of freedom from the last century now teaches a palatable history in its schools that turns a blind eye to its unique and crucial role in fighting against evil at a national level: public school teachers are dropping controversial subjects such as the Holocaust and the Crusades from history lessons because they do not want to cause offence" [5] to Muslim children.

The fear to offend Muslims or raise objections to certain tenets of the Muslim faith, however justified, must not stop us from freely speaking our minds. There was a time when the world responded appropriately to men and women who denied that the horrors of Nazi evil: with outrage. That time, unfortunately, has passed. As our friends in Europe set a precedent of silencing public concern and debate to avoid offending Muslims we must ask the question: At what price our freedom?

Perhaps the following anecdote illustrates just how well the game of political correctness can be played to silence opposition to Islam. In January of 2009 a member of the British House of Lords invited Geert Wilders to a private meeting in the Palace of Westminster. She intended to invite various colleagues to a private viewing and debate of the Dutch MP's documentary *Fitna*.

As soon as the information was made known, Lord Nazir Ahmed saw to it that the meeting was cancelled when he arranged a meeting with the Government Chief Whip of the House of Lords and Leader of the House of Lords, together with representatives from the Muslim Council of Britain, British Muslim Forumand other representatives from the British Muslim community.[6] Lord Ahmed threatened to mobilize 10,000 Muslims to prevent Mr. Wilders from entering the House and also threatened legal action against the baroness who arranged the screening of the film. As a result, the scheduled viewing of *Fitna* was cancelled and was not screened or discussed on 29 January, 2009, as had been planned. Lord Ahmed told the Pakastani press upon the meeting's cancellation that the decision was a "victory for the Muslim community."[7]

On 12 February, 2009 Wilders was invited once more to present his film in the British House of Lords. Ahmed once again stirred up opposition among Muslims. What happened next seems almost too bizarre to be true in a so-called free and democratic society. Arriving in Britain at the invitation of the British government, Wilders was arrested at Heathrow airport, detained and then deported back to Holland. The Islamic community threatened to flood the streets with angry Muslims and once again prevented the public debate it considered unacceptable, and in so doing took more ground in the war of ideas in the name of political correctness.

A British parliament whose liberties were secured through centuries of religious tolerance now buckled to the demands of the most intolerant force on earth. New precedents are being set to protect Islam. While Muslims threaten to riot over film screenings, imams openly preach hate from mosques across Britain and unlike Wilders, have free access and entry to the country. The British government allows the terrorist organization Hamas to stage huge demonstrations and do not stop Jihadi fundamentalists from openly recruiting on British university campuses. What is more, Prime Minister Gordon Brown has said that he wants to make London the center of world Islamic banking. The price the Prime Minister and the rest of Britain may have to pay for allowing such freedom for fundamentalist Islam to take root in the country may be of greater cost to Britain than the famous capitulation by then Prime Minister Chamberlain to the Nazis before the Second World War.[8] The road of political correctness is a cowardly path stripped of any clear ethic or belief in things that are right and things that are wrong. For Britain it will lead to the end of the United Kingdom we once knew. It is the same for the rest of the Western world.

THE CANADIAN CHARTER OF SOME RIGHTS AND FREEDOMS

Mark Steyn, a Canadian journalist, writes in his book *America Alone*, that we ought to be cautious of how the timid media portray world events. Citing the 2005 riots in France when immigrants, the majority young Muslims, actively showed their discontent with life in the slums, he wrote:

> Actually, I don't think everything is about Jihad. But I do think, as I said, that a good 90 percent of everything's about demography. Take that media characterization of those French rioters: "Youths." What's the salient point about youths? They're youthful. Very few octogenarians want to go torching Renaults every night. It's not easy lobbing a Molotov cocktail into a police station and then hobbling back to your walker across the street before the searing heat of the explosion melts your hip replacement. Civil disobedience is a young man's game.[9]

Steyn has come under fire for his examination of the cultural demographics of Europe, and for announcing the end of the world as we know it: "The Muslim world has youth, numbers and global ambitions. The West is growing old and enfeebled, and lacks the will to rebuff those who would supplant it."[10]

It's this kind of writing style that has put Steyn in the watchful eye of the Canadian Human Rights Commission, which seems to no longer be in the business of supporting free-speech, but looks, instead, to be in the business of defending particular groups. Some argue it has become an enabling arm of the Islamic agenda of Sharia law and state dhimitude.

Such an assault against our personal freedoms was overcome in the past on foreign soil by the precious lives of thousands of Canadian soldiers.

The current attack on freedom of speech in Canada is no small matter. In the introduction to *The Tyranny of Nice*, Steyn, who is known as much for his witty and controversial writing style as he is for the complaint filed against him by the Canadian Islamic Congress for hate speech, writes:

> In its determination to enforce a dubious government-mandated "niceness", key elements of the Canadian state have taken a jackhammer to the cornerstone of a free society: freedom of expression, freedom of ideas, freedom of belief, freedom to engage in the whole messy rough'n'tumble of vigorous debate that distinguishes open societies from lesser, stunted, insecure ones. [11]

Steyn wrote the above words after a long drawn-out examination by the Ontario Human Rights Commission and the Canadian Human Rights Commission because of the article "The Future Belongs to Islam" that he wrote for *Maclean's* magazine. In the article, Steyn predicts how an enfeebled West will be supplanted by a thriving Muslim world. Here is a sample of the writing that caused offence, and allegedly violated human rights:

> Sept. 11, 2001, was not "the day everything changed," but the day that revealed how much had already changed. On Sept. 10, how many journalists had the Council of American-Islamic Relations or the Canadian Islamic Congress or the Muslim Council of Britain in their Rolodexes? If you'd said that whether something does

or does not cause offence to Muslims would be the early 21st century's principal political dynamic in Denmark, Sweden, the Netherlands, Belgium, France and the United Kingdom, most folks would have thought you were crazy. Yet on that Tuesday morning the top of the iceberg bobbed up and toppled the Twin Towers.[12]

Although the OHRC, chaired by Jennifer Lynch, refused to rule on the complaint, stating it did not have the jurisdiction to deal with matters in magazines, it publicly condemned the writing as Islamaphobic, and unfair, biased journalism. Heavily criticized by various members of the media for pronouncing wrongdoing without holding a public hearing, providing evidence, or allowing a defence, the Commission defended its statement, stating, "Like racial profiling and other types of discrimination, ascribing the behaviour of individuals to a group damages everyone in that group. We have always spoken out on such issues. *Maclean's* and its writers are free to express their opinions. The OHRC is mandated to express what it sees as unfair and harmful comment or conduct that may lead to discrimination."[13] What is so troubling about this scenario is the Commission's staunch condemnation of free speech and its commitment to validate the claim of wrongdoing by the Islamic Congress with virtually no questions asked. The Congress said jump and the Commission jumped; pulled the violation of rights card, and the Commission followed suit.

After the dust settled, Steyn wrote about the experience:

I've learned a lot of lessons during my time in the crosshairs of the Lynch mob. Although the feistier columnists have spoken out on this issue, the broad mass of Canadian media seems generally indifferent to a power grab that explicitly threatens to reduce them to a maple-flavoured variant of Pravda. One boneheaded "journalism professor" even attempted to intervene in the British Columbia trial on the side of the censors. As some leftie website put it, "Defending freedom of speech for jerks means defending jerks." Well, yes. But, in this case, not defending the jerks means not defending freedom of speech for yourself. It's not a left/right thing; it's a free/unfree thing. But an alarming proportion of the Dominion's "media workers" seem relatively relaxed about playing the role of eunuchs to the Trudeaupian sultans.[14]

The entire episode suggests the Charter of Human Rights in Canada could easily become a Charter of *Certain* Rights and Freedoms. The case before the OHRC serves as an example of intimidation to those who would speak their mind and disagree with Islam. It also displays how easy it is to cry wolf: there is little personal cost to drop a hate speech bomb on someone exercising their right to speak freely, however the fall out for the one accused is explosive, with damage to personal reputation and great personal cost. Those who cry wolf may be dressed in sheep's clothing, but beware the real wolves. We cannot forget that there is a real agenda by certain Muslims to Islamatize the world.

THE HAMMER OF GOD

Earlier in the book I trace the steps of Muhammad on his one-man journey into the cave. An illiterate who was not capable of reading the words he claimed were false in the scriptures became the father of a whole theology. Upon Muhammad's revelation came slaughter, and after

Muhammad's death, Islam experienced 100 years of unbelievable success in many tremendous victories. Its brutal means of conquest nearly wiped out all of the Christian world, until 732, when a large army of Islamic conquerors invaded the kingdom of the Franks, a land known later as France. They were defeated at the Battle of Tours by Charles Martel.

Martel's army was composed of a few thousand knights and some local farmers armed only with the scythes they used to harvest their grain. Martel's fearsome and capable warriors, familiar with the geography and climate of the region halted the Muslim invasion in what historians describe as "one of the most decisive battles in European and Christian history."[115] If God had not granted the victory, the whole Western world would now be speaking Arabic and bowing toward Mecca.

The victory of Martel had everything to do with tactic. The leader of the Muslim army staged a "wild, headlong charge continually repeated" with men on swift horses armed with javelins and short swords. The onslaught was "very wasteful of men."[16] Martel's men were armed with spears, battle axes and great two-edged swords. They formed a phalanx standing shoulder to shoulder and, as the chronicler Isidore of Beja records, "stood motionless like a wall of ice." [17] The chronicle of the battle reveals that the Franks cut down invading men and horse alike until "the road and surrounding fields were choked with corpses." The leader of the invading horde was killed in the course of the battle, and the Islamic force fled. The Chronicle of Saint Denis says of Charles Martel, "As a hammer of iron, of steel, and of every other metal, even so he dashed and smote in the battle all his enemies."[18]

I believe the Battle of Tours is one of the many well kept secrets of Christian history. It does not fit into what I now understand as the endlessly misguided principles of our contemporary Christian faith. Somehow pacifism is a DNA doctrine, a deep part of our current Christian psyche in the West. I am often bewildered and shocked to realize how much of the Christian world has been forever wiped out by the onslaught of Islam. Simply look at the multitude of nations that incorporate the Crescent Moon into their nation's flag. These countries have a spiritual allegiance to their Moon deity, Allah, and loyally follow their prophet Muhammad, subscribing to his doctrine for life, as taught in the Qur'an.

Hundreds of years ago, when attacked by radical Muslims who meant to pillage and wipe out his people, the forgotten, powerful leader, Charles the Hammer had to respond with decisive force. His unmovable army slaughtered the Islamic warriors, who were drunk with power and plunder, and had not lost in battle for 100 years. Although Muslim forces would remain for years in areas of southern France, the battle "effectively marked the end of Muslim expansion in the west."[19] Note that Martel's tactic was not pacifism or turning the other cheek. He faced the attacking armies, who meant to destroy his way of life, and handed them defeat, unflinchingly. Martel kept no prisoners and allowed no survivors, except for those who fled before him. The battle was so fierce and so thorough that it changed the face of Islam for the next 450 years and stopped its further spread through Europe.

I SEE PICTURES

Earlier this year, my daughter and her family found their much-loved German Shepherd dead in their driveway. The family prepared a burial site and wrapped the dog in a blanket and said goodbye to the faithful companion. My six year-old granddaughter asked her mother who would protect her now from bad men or coyotes on the acreage where they live. She was understandably alarmed and afraid, saddened at the dog's death. A few days after the dog died my granddaughter dreamt that the dog dug his way out of his grave and returned to life. But in the dream he only lived for a little while and then died once again. As she talked with her mother about her dream she was quiet for a while and then she said, "This was a bad dream because it came with the pictures." Asking what she meant, my daughter asked "Do you mean you see the pictures in your mind about your dream?" A little six year-old child had to learn the reality of life and death, and was haunted in her dreams. My heart breaks to imagine her fragile voice telling her mother, "I see pictures."

Like my granddaughter, I am haunted by pictures. But the ones I see are not from a dream. I see the documentary pictures of a screaming kidnapped victim held in the gleeful hands of Muslim captors as they begin to crudely decapitate their prisoner, and finally hold up his severed head, blood dripping to the ground as they shout Aluha Akbar!

I see a woman hauled into the desert by jeering, shouting, men. The woman covered from head to toe in a burqa has been charged, without evidence, by her husband for commiting adultery. A hole is dug in the ground and she is placed in the shallow depth so that she cannot fall over. A sadistic stoning ritual begins. Soon the white garment turns red with blood and the howling cries of the men cannot be contained as they throw stones viciously pound the spirit right out of her body.

I see a journalist who has paid his way into a Taliban-controlled village on the Pakistani-Afghan border. His camera crew is busy recording a group of smiling Taliban, who proudly show off their modern weaponry and allow a picture to be taken of a demolished school for girls. The female teacher, they brag, has been shot and killed and the girls banished back to their homes. "Allah rules here!" they shout in jubilation. "Death to Israel! Death to the USA!"

I see a Nigerian Christian convert from Islam who is captured by his Muslim neighbors, beaten mercilessly, then crucified and left to die in the night. But in the morning he is still alive, so they take a hot iron and press it into his hands until they become a bloody mass of flesh and bone. They stuff his anus with burning peppers and drag him into the bush to be consumed by animals. He is later rescued by nearby villagers and lives. I look at his photo taken years later, and will never forget his scarred and devastated hands.

I see Muslim men and women shouting death threats to anyone who dares to offend the prophet on streets in Canada. Women dressed in full black from head to toe, faces covered, shouting obscenities aimed at Israel. "Build bigger ovens," they scream. Men with their necks wrapped in PLO scarves are foaming at the mouth with vitriol hatred. They would kill innocent women and children without hesitation if given the chance. A beautiful girl, the age of my own granddaughter, is asked what she would do if President Bush was in front of her and she had a knife. She screams in her tiny voice, "I would kill him!" She's asked, "What do you know about Jews?" Without missing a beat she screams, "They are apes and pigs!"

I see these pictures, of what Islam preaches and the fruit it produces. And yet it seems most people do not see the same pictures as I do. Many Christians today seem passively detached from the history of the Muslim faith and ongoing events. They happily live lives of comfort of ease in the West and tune out things that matter by tuning in to the entertainment and information the main stream media feeds them. We make the Beast we are to dread and resist feel welcome and at home. We are told to love our enemies and do good to them that hate us. Does loving our enemies mean we adopt or celebrate their values and worldview?

In a recent issue of the *Banner,* the monthly magazine published by the Christian Reformed Church of North America, a picture displayed a large group of Korean Christians visiting Jerusalem to learn more about the history of their faith. The photograph showed the Christians in front of the Dome of the Rock, one of Islam's most prominent and recognizable structures. To me the image of Christians in front of the Muslim place of worship, a typical tourist photograph, carries with it a sense of tragic irony and borders on spiritual pornography.

In an earlier chapter I explained the vision of Muhammad's night journey, from where he ascended into heaven on a strange horse-like creature and met a freckled, red haired Jesus along with Moses and others. The place where this purported vision occurred was at the place where the Dome of the Rock was eventually built, to celebrate the momentous occasion. But one has to realize and recognize the significance of the ground on which the Dome of the Rock is built. It sits on the site of the where the Jewish Temple used to stand, before it was destructed, once for all, by Rome in 70 AD: Mount Zion.

Ellis Skolfield, in his book *False Prophet*, examines Daniel 11: 31: "His armed forces will rise up to desecrate the temple fortress and will abolish the daily sacrifice. Then they will set up the abomination that causes desolation." Skolfield notes that many scholars consider the abomination referred to in Daniel to have been enacted by Antiochus Epiphanes in 168 BC. He devastated Jerusalem and offered a pig on the altar in the Temple, desecrating it. For Skolfield, the great abomination of the temple is none other than the eye-catching Dome of the Rock, which sits on the most Holy historical site of biblical history.[20] The fact that it shines brighter than anything else in the Holy city of Jerusalem should remind us that it is a beautiful site of evil. Whether Skolfield's interpretation of Daniel is accurate or not is for theologians to decide. However I do respect his view that the Muslim place of worship is more of a desecration than it is a place of holiness; more an abomination than a picturesque photo-op, which is what many Christian pilgrims to the Holy Land view it as.

The Dome of the Rock is a symbol and historical example of the sword of Islam sweeping across the earth, claiming territory and holy land. The great and present danger we face in the West today is the personal freedoms that were part of our foundation as nations being swept away by ideology and worldview opposed to our Christian faith. We have witnessed the annihilation of the Protestant faith in our public schools, replaced by Human Secularism. And we see the tolerance and political correctness this ideology preaches pave the way for the Islamization of the West.

In some ways, the fears and concerns people have in our times are mostly now about the hard financial times we find ourselves in with the current economic issues worldwide. The fear of Islamic terrorism seems far removed from our thoughts; out of sight and out of mind. The spread of Islam has not stopped. If anything it increases, however, subtle through the jihad of Sharia finance. Muslims are spreading their beliefs. I have seen it in my own community. The dispensation of Muslim values is shrewd as Muslims are entering conversation with free-thinking Westerners, connecting with people in the places they live their lives: through churches, college campuses, and in communities. The mission, mandate, and final purpose of Islam has been the same for the past 1400 years and will continue to be until the end of the age.

My prayer that each of us will understand what our part is to play, that we will know also, how to unveil the threat of Islam and the cultural blindfold of political correctness.

How we respond to the veiled threat will determine what pictures our grandchildren will see.

AUTHOR'S NOTE

The stage of human history is set for war and we live on a battleground. Good and evil meet in fierce battle in heaven and on the earth. We must understand the times. We must read the signs. The Trade towers in New York, bombings in Madrid and London, the horrors of Sudan now spreading beyond that devastated country's borders toward Chad; the hatred spewed from Iran, the burning of hundreds of newly built schools in Afghanistan, the fear to offend Muslims in Europe, the Middle East, in North America: these are some of the signs that tell me the eve of the next Great War is upon us.

I hear the same voices sounded in the 1930s before the Second World War adamantly denying the possibility of an evil movement powerful enough to snuff out the life the West enjoys in our day, unwilling to believe the world could see another War or that life as we know it could ever change. Those voices of doubt in the pre-war years of the 1930s were finally silenced by the undeniable facts: Nazi death camps, bombed-out cities, a world at war. Winston Churchill was a lone voice in a wilderness of disbelief who appealed in vain to political leaders of the time to open their eyes to the growing fascist threat during the 1930s posed by Germany and Italy. He recited a poem, "The Clattering Train," to characterize the failure of his government in 1935 to re-arm:

> Those in charge of the clattering train, the axles creak
> and the couplings strain.
> The pace is hot and the points are near and sleep has
> deadened the driver's air.
> The signals flash in the night in vain, for death is in
> charge of the clattering train.[1]

Good triumphed over evil by the grace of God. The Allies won the war. From our vantage point in history we see that victory and I

162

remember with great clarity the joy of my personal liberation from the Nazis in Holland in May of 1945. But as the Second World War played out, the history of the West hung in the balance and all of Europe held its breath. Victory came at a great price in millions upon millions of lives.

Put your ear to the ground. Can you hear the train clattering? We live in such a world where evil does rear its terrible head. Yet it is so easy for us to let the tangible facts of terrible evil at work in the world remain ignored because it is "far from us" in time. In the comfort and security of the times we live, peace won for us because many Allied soldiers fought the evil power that threatened to pull our way of life from us, it is easy to forget that life was not always so peaceful or that security came at a great price. We also turn a blind eye to the terrible evil at work in places far away. We know, for example, of the horrendous human tragedies in the Sudan. They are well documented and fully recognized by the United Nations. Yet the slaughter of countless innocents continues. The world can no longer claim "We did not know!" as so many claimed after World War II. And yet it does little to bring change. We have heard of the mass graves, of entire villages wiped out, that millions of people are displaced, that women are held in internment camps and systematically raped by government soldiers to put an end to the pure bloodlines of entire tribes. But the horror is so far away, it is almost unreal.

Though the enemy wears different clothes and wields different weapons, even calls upon a different god, it is that same Enemy. But so few are willing to see or admit that evil is real, breathing down our necks.

Whether we believe it or not, as we go about our daily lives, the eternal struggle between good and evil continues as it has since the beginning of human time. And we, insignificant individuals and nations as we seem, live out a drama that has profound meaning in the unfolding of history.

Pinch yourself. It is real. You are in the middle of the war. It is a battle that has been fought and won before. What part will you play?

FOOTNOTES

CHAPTER 1

1. Nancy Gibbs. *One nation: America Remembers September 11, 2001*. New York: Little, Brown and Company, 2001, 174.
2. ibid.
3. Revelations 12:7
4. see Zechariah 3:1 and John 8:44-45
5. John Milton. *Paradise Lost* . Ed. Scott Elledge. New York: W.W. Norton & Company. 1993. 145-46.
6. John Eldridge. *Epic*. Nashville: Thomas Nelson Inc., 2001. 12-13
7. ibid, 14.
8. Swain, Diana (Host). (2004). In *CBC News World*: CBC Television. 6-9 Dec.
9. Jean Hudon, "The Empire of Darkness Series #25: Torture and Other Human Rights Abuse." Available: http://www.earthrainbownetwork. com/Archives2005/EmpireDarkness25.htm.
10. Andrew Sullivan. "Yes, America Has Changed." 1 September, 2002. *Time* [On-line]. Available: www.time.com/time/covers/1101020909. asullivan.html
11. ibid

CHAPTER 2

1. Ted Byfield,, ed. *The S word of Islam: The Muslim Onslaught all but Destroys Christendom.* (2004). *The Christians, Their First 2000 Years* (Vol. 5). In Canada: Friesens Corporation. 39. I am greatly indebted to the scholarly work of this volume, especially for the above information about the People of the Camel.
2. ibid.
3. ibid.
4. ibid, 45
5. ibid
6. Yahiya Emerick. *The Complete Idiot's Guide to Understanding Islam.* Indianapolis: Alpha, 2002. 272.

CHAPTER 3

1. *Bukhari: V4B5N73*
2. see the history of Ishmael (Arab) and Isaac (Israel) in Genesis 16 – 25 and Galatians 4
3. Dr. Anis A. Shorrosh. *Islam Revealed*. Nashville: Thomas Nelson Publishers, 1988. 28
4. 16 July 622 is considered the first year of the Islamic calendar, see *Sword*, 56
5. These goddesses are referred to in the Quran 53:19-20
6. *Sword of Islam*, 20-24.
7. ibid, 75.
8. For example, the expulsion of Jews from Italy by the emperor Claudius in AD 49 is recorded in the book of Acts and elsewhere in history. Jews rioted because of the Christian teaching the Jesus was the Christ ("Chrestus") and Claudius would have none of it. Jews were not welcomed back to Rome until Nero, who had a half Jewish wife, came to power in AD 54. By AD 64 Christians and Jews were recognized by Rome as distinct religions: the fact that Christians were severely persecuted under Nero while Jews were exempt highlights the distinction.
9. ibid, 78.
10. Jewish scripture records that Abraham took Isaac to the mountain and records no contact between Moses and Gabriel.
11. ibid
12. Volume 5. The Christians. 'The Sword of Islam.' 71-81.
13. Understanding Islam, 198
14. *Sword of Islam*, 153.
15. ibid.
16. ibid.

CHAPTER 4

1. *Sword of Islam*, 155.
2. ibid, 24.
3. ibid, 11
4. Irshad Manji, *The Trouble with Islam*. Toronto: Random House, 2003. 49
5. Quran 2:256
6. Quran 9:29
7. Islam Revealed, 170-71.
8. *Understanding Islam*, 188-89.
9. ibid, 207.
10. 3:39-42
11. Luke 1: 65 (*Modern King James Version*)
12. Scripture records that Gabriel appeared to the prophet Daniel (c. 536 BC), to the priest Zechariah (c. 3 BC), and to the virgin Mary (c. 3 BC) see Daniel 8:16 and 9:21; Luke 1:19; 26.
13. Luke 1:5-22
14. see St. Luke's preface to the work written under the commission of Theophilus, the Roman official, in Luke 1:1-4. Luke 11:9 and John 8:32
15. Quran 2:2-8; see also *Understanding Islam*, 232.
16. Quran, 9:5
17. Joel Richardson. *Will Islam Be Our Future?* Available: www.answering-islam.org.uk/Authors/JR/Future/ch16_understanding_dishonesty.htm
18. *Sword of Islam*, 84
19. ibid, 9
20. Exodus 34:6-7
21. G.K. Chesterton, *The Everlasting Man*. 1925. San Francisco: Ignatius Press, 1993. 202, 204.
22. ibid, 207.
23. Luke 6:35

Chapter 5

1. Matthew 4:1-11
2. *Trouble*, 40.
3. 2:100-106
4. Kingdom of the Cults, PAGE?
5. John 4:19-23
6. see article 15 of the Charter
7. *Understanding Islam*
8. ibid.
9. ibid

Chapter 6

1. *Bukhari* V4B52N220
2. "Iranians say Israel spat is really about nukes." From MSNBC News Services Updated: 11:20 p.m. ET Oct. 30, 2005. Posted at: http://www.msnbc.msn.com/id/9823624
3. The above quotes are found, respectively, in *Quran* 2:61, 2:64, 4:55, 5:14, 9:29ff, 17:7, 33:26
4. *Trouble With Islam*
5. *Trouble*
6. *Quran* 5:59
7. Vancouver B.C. Muslim cleric Sheik Kathadra
8. Carl Cantrell. "Al-taqiyya." Available online: http://www.hauns.com/~DCQu4E5g/koran5.html.
9. *Understanding Islam,* from the "Introduction."
10. Brigitte Gabriel, "Message from the President and Founder." Available online: http://www.americancongressfortruth.com
11. Phyllis Chesler, *The New Anti-Semitism.*
12. Craig Winn. *Prophet of Doom.* Available online: http://www.prophetofdoom.net/
13. Walter Martin. *Kingdom of the Cults.* PAGE?
14. "Types of Human Rights Violations. *Faith and Belief in Sudan in the Midst of Persecution, Slavery, and Genocide.* Available: http://home.earthlink.net/~drbettyh/Sudanpage.htm#types
15. ibid.
16. ibid.
17. ibid.
18. *Trouble,* 10
19. Quran 4:35
20. *Trouble,* 50. See also *Quran* 2:224: "Women are your fields, go into your fields when you please. Do good works and please God."
21. ibid, 50.
22. From, "Inside the Mind of a Suicide Bomber" at http://cedarmailer.com/americancongress/pages/archive/messagedetails.asp?ID=504
23. "Inside the Mind of a Suicide Bomber"
24. *ibid*
25. "The micropolitics of identity/difference: Recognition and

accommodation in everyday life" Available at: http://www.findarticles.com/p/articles/mi_qa3671/is_200010/ai_n8910362

26. ibid
27. Daniel Pipes quotes Zein Isa in Ellen Harris' book *Guarding the Secrets: Palestinian Terrorism and a Father's Murder of His Too-American Daughter* on his blogsite at: http://www.danielpipes.org/article/672
28. "USA V. TAWFIQ MUSA", FROM MITP TERRORIST KNOWLEDGE BASE AT http://www.tkb.org/CaseHome.jsp?caseid=307
29. Kamila Hyat, director of the Human Rights Commission of Pakistan, quoted in "15-year-old girl flees in fear of honour killing" in a *Daily Times/Reuters* article posted at Pakistan Facts webpage.
30. ibid
31. ibid
32. *Trouble*, 154.
33. 4:16
34. *Trouble*
35. Gregory Smith, *The River War*, first edition, Vol. II. London: Longmans, Green & Co., 1899, 248-50.
36. Islam Revealed, 180 quoting Osborn's, Life of Mahomet
37. ibid

CHAPTER 7

1. Walter Martin. *Kingdom of the Cults*, 443.
2. Douglas Montero and Stefan C. Friedman. "'Islamic Hate' Eyed in Slays; Christian PA Got E-Threats Before massacre." *New York Post*. New York, N.Y.: Jan 16, 2005. pg. 007
3. ibid
4. Quran 47:4
5. The passage continues to inform men what to do about women suspected of being disloyal and of ill conduct : "at first refuse to share your bed with them and finally beat them." See Quran 3:034. In a democratic society, who decides when and how women are disloyal and of ill conduct?
6. see Brigitte Gabriel's interview with French Filmmaker Pierre Rehov concerning his film *Suicide Killers*, available online at: http://cedarmailer.com/americancongress/pages/archive/messagedetails. asp?ID=504; see also Rehov's film *Hostages of Hatred* as well as Congressman Eric Cantor on the subject
7. Osama Bin Laden's now infamous claim and reasoning for the attacks.
8. Daniel Pipes. "[Theo van Gogh and] "Education By Murder" in Holland" *New York Sun*. November 16, 2004, from http://www. danielpipes.org/article/2218; see also "Gunman Kills Dutch Film Director" from BBC NEWS:http://news.bbc.co.uk/go/pr/fr/-/1/ hi/world/europe/3974179.stm Published: 2004/11/02 11:41:02 GMT
9. "Slaughter And 'Submission.'" *CBS News*. March 13, 2005. Available online: http://www.cbsnews.com/stories/2005/03/11/60minutes/ main679609.shtml
10. Happy Feder. "Scary, Scary Night." Available online: http:// cedarmailer.com/americancongress/pages/archive/messagedetails. asp?ID=5

CHAPTER 8

1. David Frum. *An End To Evil*. New York: Random House, 2003. 157.
2. *Understanding Islam*, 31.
3. ibid.
4. "Iran president wants Israel 'wiped off the map.'" Associated Press. October 26, 2005. Available online: www.msnbc.com/id/9823624.
5. Brigitte Gabrielle. "Welcome Message." American Congress for Truth. November 2005. Available online http://www.americancongressfortruth.com/
6. *Orthodoxy*, 121

CHAPTER 9

1. Joseph Farah. "Al-Qaida's Most Likely Nuke Targets." Available online: www.g2.wnd.com
2. ibid, quoting from the book *The al-Qaida Connection: International Terrorism, Organized Crime and the Coming Apocalypse* by Paul L. Williams.
3. *Islam revealed*, 172.
4. D.C. Watson, "Islam, The West's Unmanageable Liability," American Congress for Truth at http://cedarmailer.com/americancongress/pages/archive/messagedetails.asp?ID=222

Chapter 10

1. Gilbert. K. Chesterton. *Heretics*. 1919 edition published by the John Lane Company of New York City and printed by the Plimpton Press of Norwood, Massachusetts, taken from the Guttenberg Project Online.
2. Ephesians 6:11
3. Matthew 10:16
4. Brigitte Gabriel. "Have the Presbyterians Lost Their Conscience?" June 17th, 2006. Online: http://cedarmailer.com/americancongress/pages/archive/messagedetails.asp?ID=460
5. *Understanding Islam*, 107-108.
6. "Why is it hard for Muslims to believe in Christ as their Savior?" Dan Vander Lugt. Available at http://www.rbc.org
7. Matthew 18:20
8. "Inside the Mind of a Suicide Bomber"
9. "Merkel warns against bowing to fear of Muslim violence," Madeline Chambers Wed Sep 27, 2006, at http://today.reuters.com/news/articlenews.aspx?type=worldNews&storyid=2006-09-27T164143Z_01_L27167228_RTRUKOC_0_US-GERMANY-MUSLIMS.xml&src=rss&rpc=22
10. "Pope 'deeply sorry' for comments on Islam: Muslims greet pontiff's apology with mixed reaction," Associated Press Sept 17, 2006, at http://www.msnbc.msn.com/id/14871562/
11. ibid
12. "Nun shot dead as apology by Pope fails to quell the violence." Stephen McGinty, Mon 18 Sep 2006, The Scotsman, at http://news.scotsman.com/index.cfm?id=1377592006
13. "Pope deeply sorry"
14. "Fear of Offending Islam Spurs Hot Debate in Europe" By Mark Trevelyan and Mike Collett-White, at http://today.reuters.com/news/articlenews.aspx?type=newsOne&storyID=2006-09-27T172654Z_01_L27153067_RTRUKOC_0_US-ARTS-RELIGION.xml&src=092706_1428_ARTICLE_PROMO_also_on_reuters
15. "Merkel"
16. David Young in a speech to the annual conference of think-tank

Oxford Analytica, September 2006, see "Fear of Islam Spurs Hot Debate in Europe."

17. "Fear of Offending Islam Spurs Hot Debate in Europe"
18. Ephesians 6:12
19. "Because the Hate," Jamie Glazov, FrontPagemag.com; September 25, 2006
20. see "Because they Hate" as well as http://www.frontpagemag.com/websat/Helper/editor/www.freedomhouse.org/religion for the Freedom House report
21. "Because they Hate"

CHAPTER 11

1. Revelation 22:18-20
2. *Orthodoxy*, 105.
3. *Understanding Islam*, 107-108
4. "The Coming of the Mystery Imam al Mahdi" Sunday Times (Colombo, Sri Lanka) Nov.18, 1990.
5. In Ezekiel 38: 1-6 the prophet pronounces judgment against these nations, perhaps once belonging to Eastern Asia Minor. In the book of Revelation, the nations symbolically represent nations that are against Christians, the people of God.
6. In the book of Revelation, the Beast and the False Prophet have symbolically represented governments and religions, respectively, throughout the Church Age opposed to the Kingdom of God. From a Biblical perspective, Islam and its prophet seem to fit the description today.
7. Revelation 20: 1-10

CHAPTER 12

1. Alex Alexiev, "What Is Sharia Finance? Don't Ask the Treasury" *Human Events*, November 12, 2008. Avaliable at http://www. humanevents.com/
2. ibid
3. ibid
4. ibid
5. Andrew C. McCarthy, "Pirates Test the 'Rule of Law,' " *The National Review Online*, April 10, 2009. Available at http://www. nationalreview.com/
6. ibid

CHAPTER 13

1. "Islam film Dutch MP to be charged," *BBC Online*, 21 January 2009. Available at http://news.bbc.co.uk/2/hi/europe/7842344. stm

2. "Geert Wilders prosecuted for hate speech, " *NRC Handelsblad*, 21 January 2009. Available at http://www.nrc.nl/international/article2126874.ece

3. ibid

4. "Islam film"

5. Alexandra Frean, "Schools drop Holocaust lessons to avoid offence," *The Times Online*, April 2, 2007. Available at http://www.timesonline.co.uk/tol/news/uk/education/article1600686.ece

6. "British Parliament calls off screening of controversial film," *Associated Press of Pakistan*. Available at http://www.app.com.pk/en_/index.php?option=com_content&task=view&id=65842&Itemid=2

7. ibid

8. see Stephen Brown. "British Government Sacrifices Free Speech On the Altar of Islamist Appeasement," *FrontPageMagazine.com*, 13 February, 2009. Available at http://www.actforamerica.org/index.php/learn/email-archives/892-british-government-capitulates-again?format=pdf

9. Mark Steyn. *America Alone*. Washington DC, Regnery Publishing, Inc. 34.

10. Mark Steyn. "The Future Belongs to Islam," *Maclean's*, 20 October, 2006.

11. *see* Steyn's introduction to *The Tyranny Of Nice* by Kathy Shaidle and Pete Vere, at *http://www.steynstore.com/product51.html*

12. Steyn, "Future Belongs to Islam."

13. "Mark Steyn," *Wikipedia*. Available at http://en.wikipedia.org/wiki/Mark_Steyn

14. ibid

15. *The Christians, Their First Two Thousand Years: The Sword of Islam.* The Christian History Project, 2004. 248.

16. ibid, 249.

17. ibid, 249.

18. ibid, 249

19. ibid, 250

20. Ellis Skolfield. *The False Prophet*. Fish House Publishing, 2001. 44. Available at http://www.ellisskolfield.com

Author's Note

1. "Dhimmitude for Dummies". Victor Sharpe. *Front Page Magazine.*
   Sept. 26, 2006. Available at http://www.frontpagemag.com/Articles/
   ReadArticle.asp?ID=24592

CPSIA information can be obtained at www.ICGtesting.com
Printed in the USA
LVOW110354091012

302010LV00001B/7/P